101 Uses for a

Dead Cat

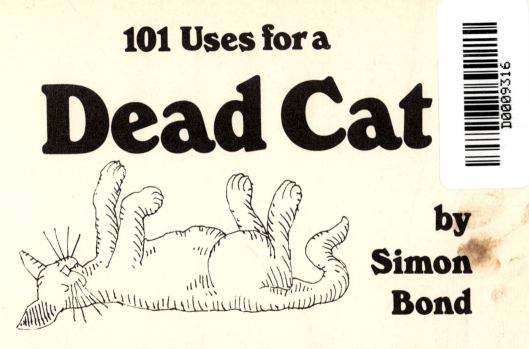

by
Simon
Bond

Clarkson N. Potter, Inc./Publishers   NEW YORK
DISTRIBUTED BY CROWN PUBLISHERS, INC.

Copyright © 1981 by Simon Bond

All rights reserved. No part of this book may be
reproduced or utilized in any form or by any means,
electronic or mechanical, including photocopying,
recording, or by any information storage and retrieval
system, without permission in writing from the
publisher.

Inquiries should be addressed to Clarkson N. Potter,
Inc., One Park Avenue, New York, New York 10016

Printed in the United States of America

Published in Great Britain by Eyre Methuen Ltd.

Library of Congress Catalog Card Number: 81-1189

ISBN: 0-517-545160

20   19   18   17   16   15   14   13   12   11

Design by: Anistatia Vassilopoulos

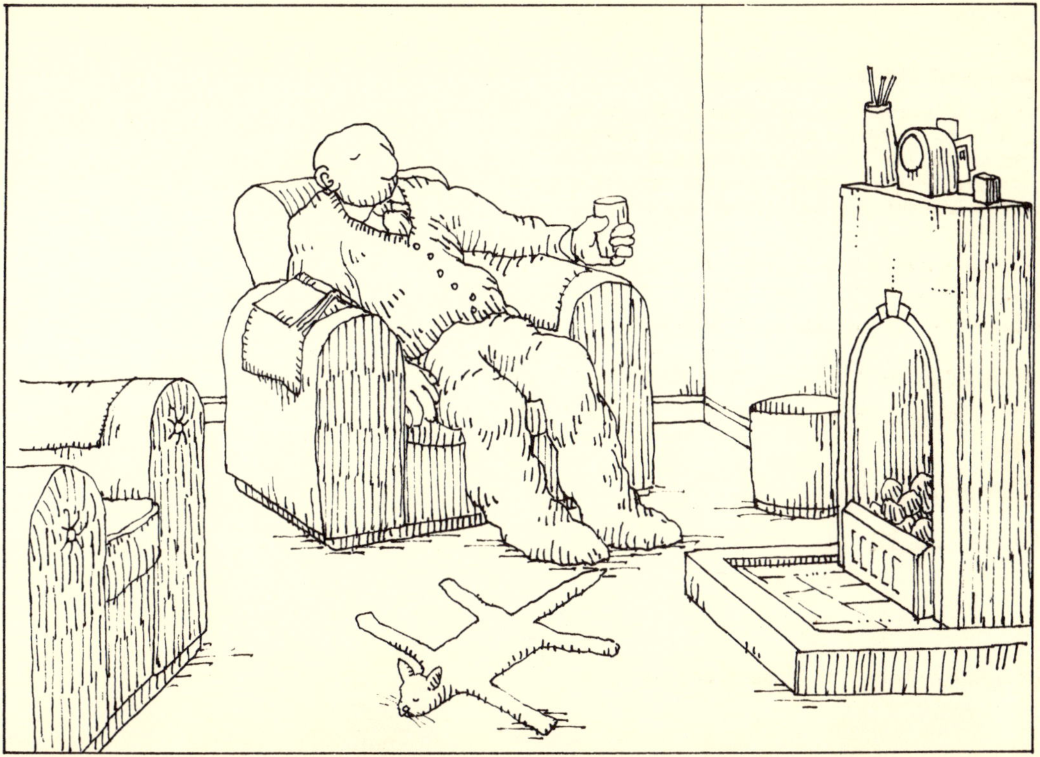

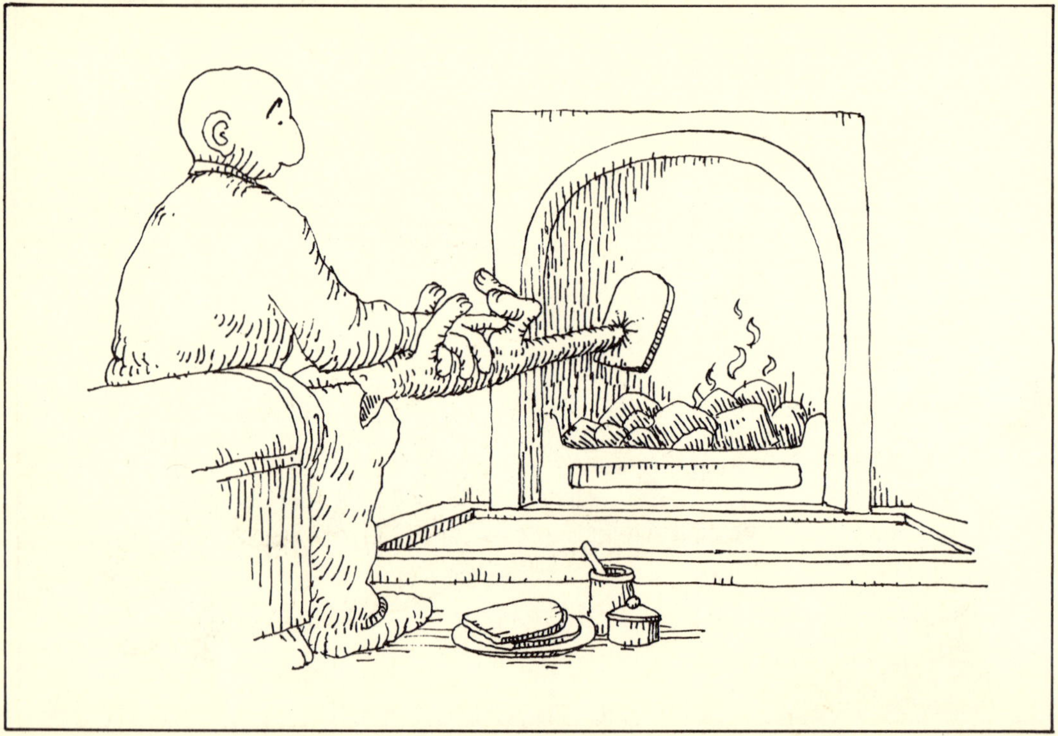

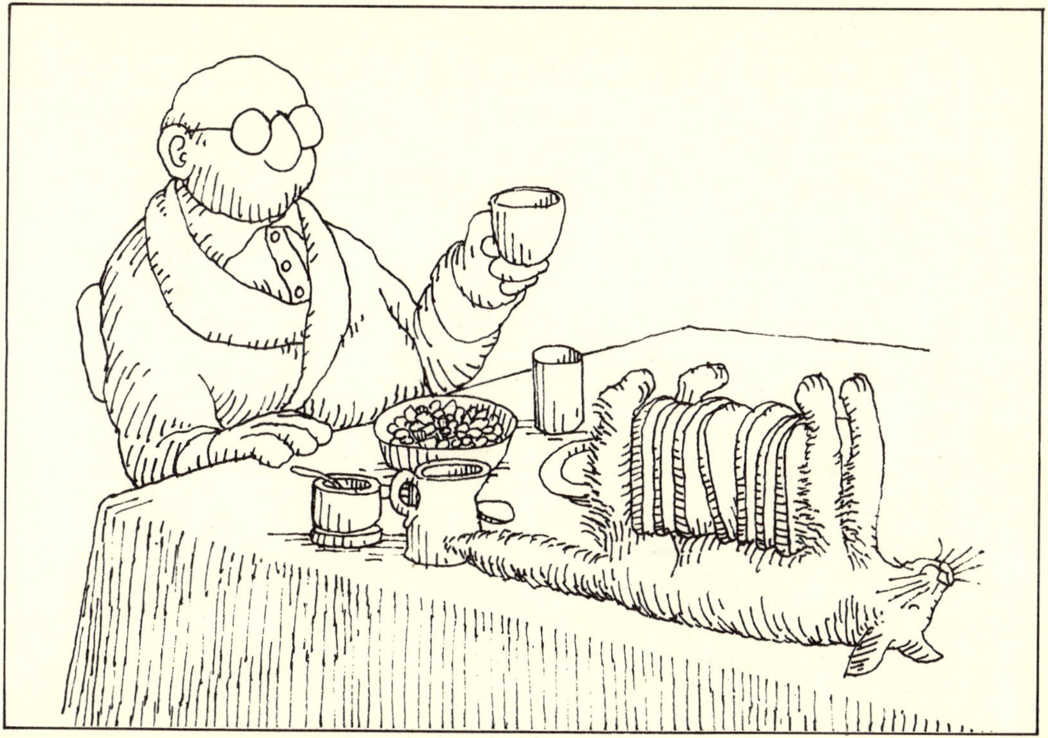

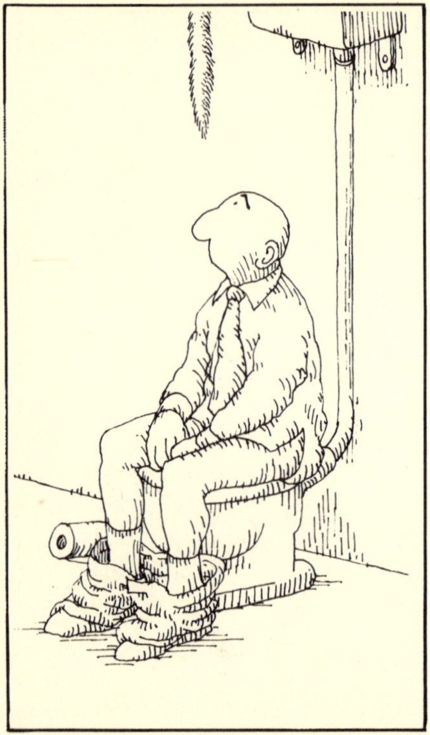

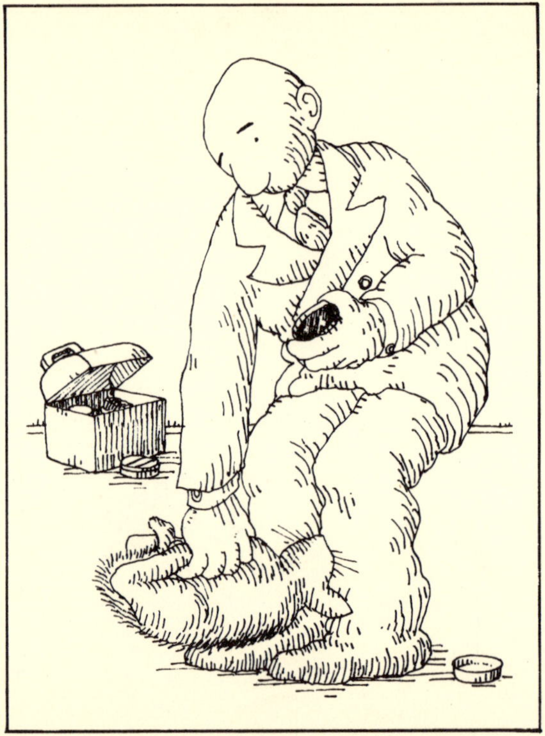

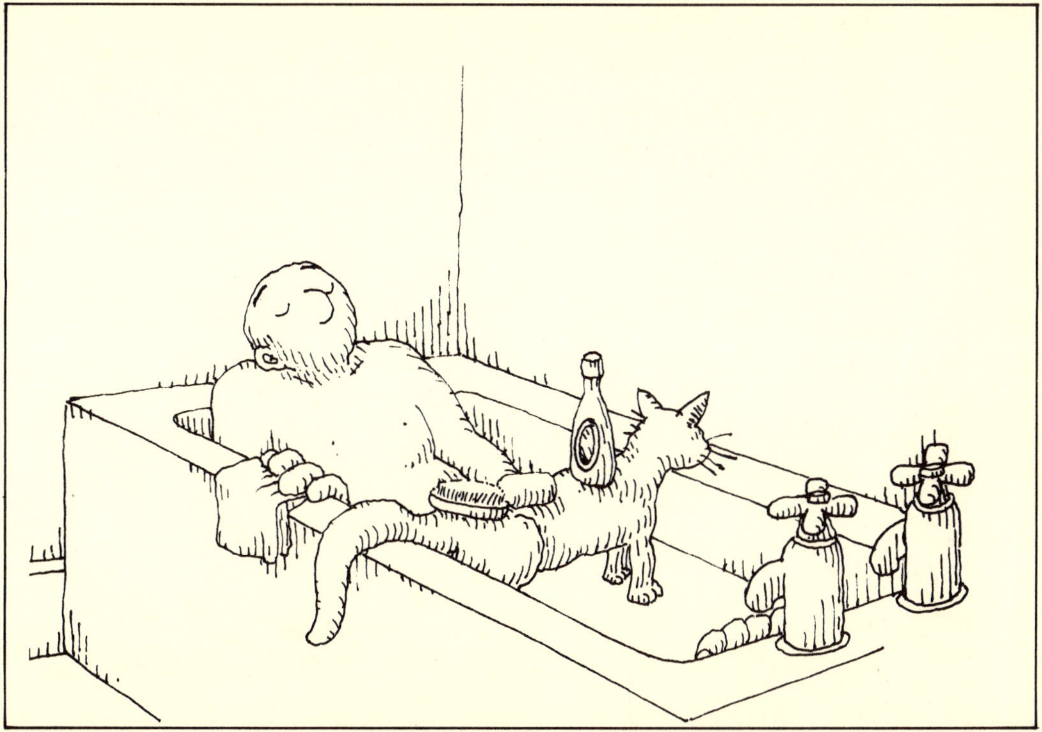

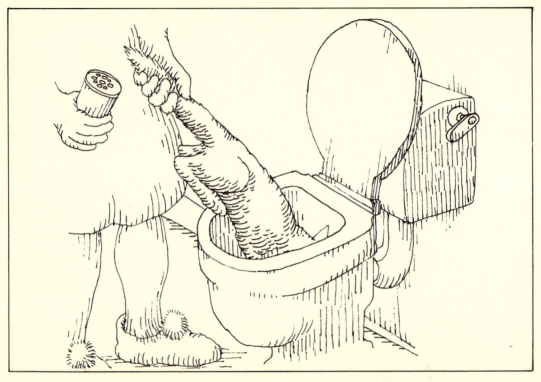

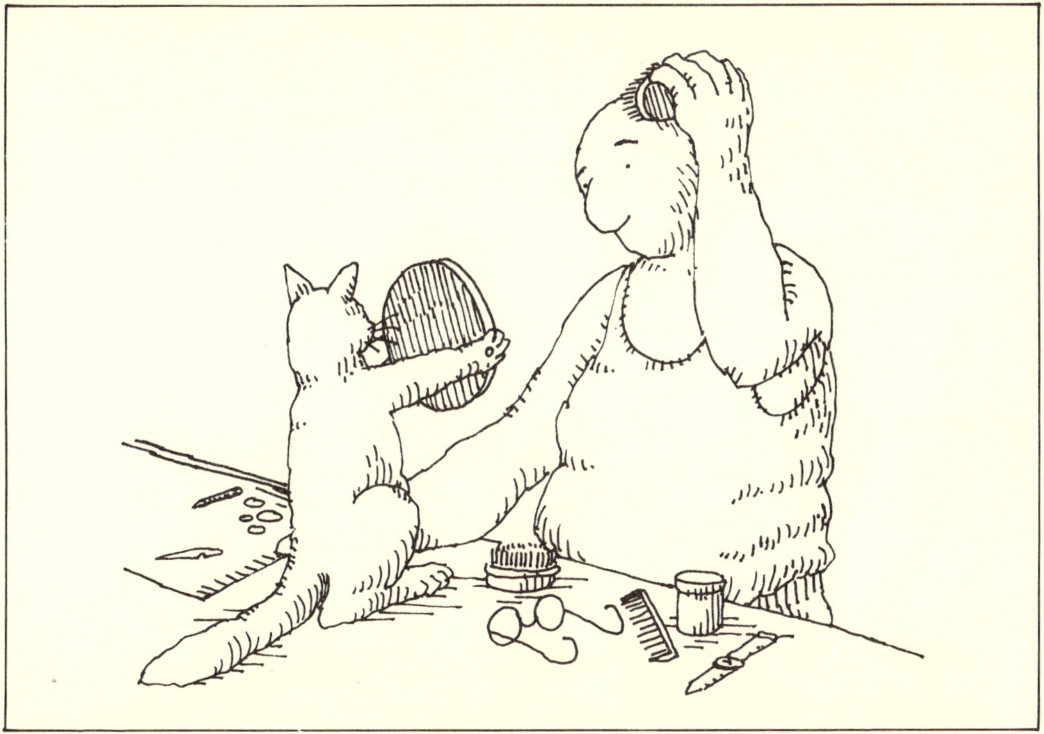

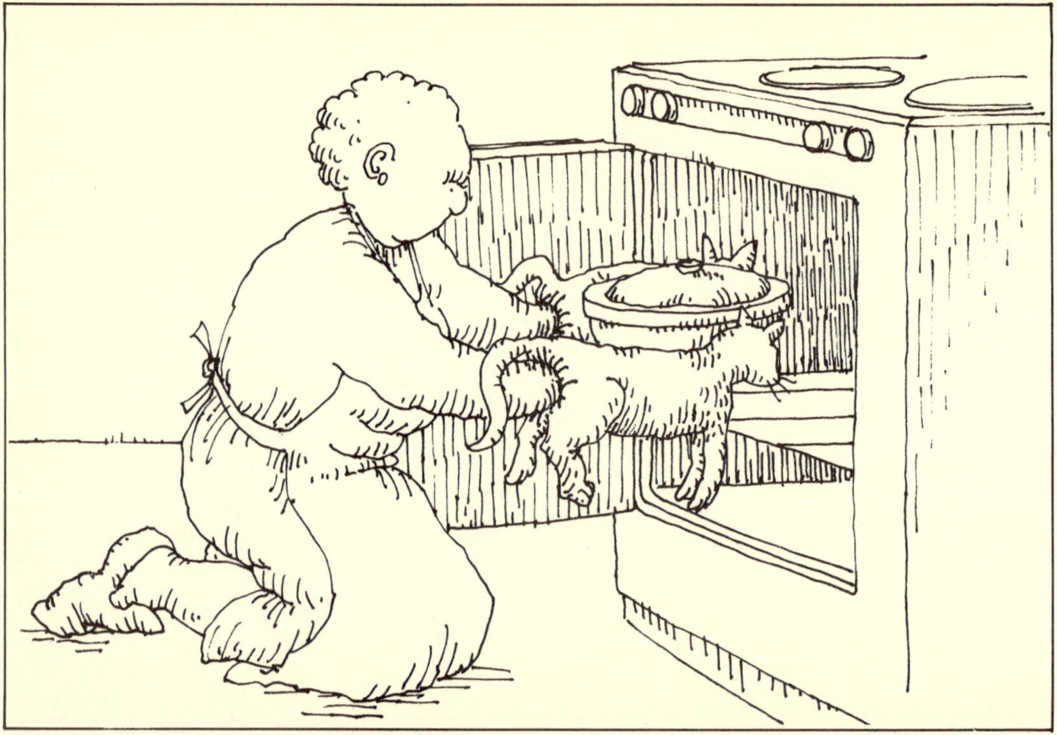

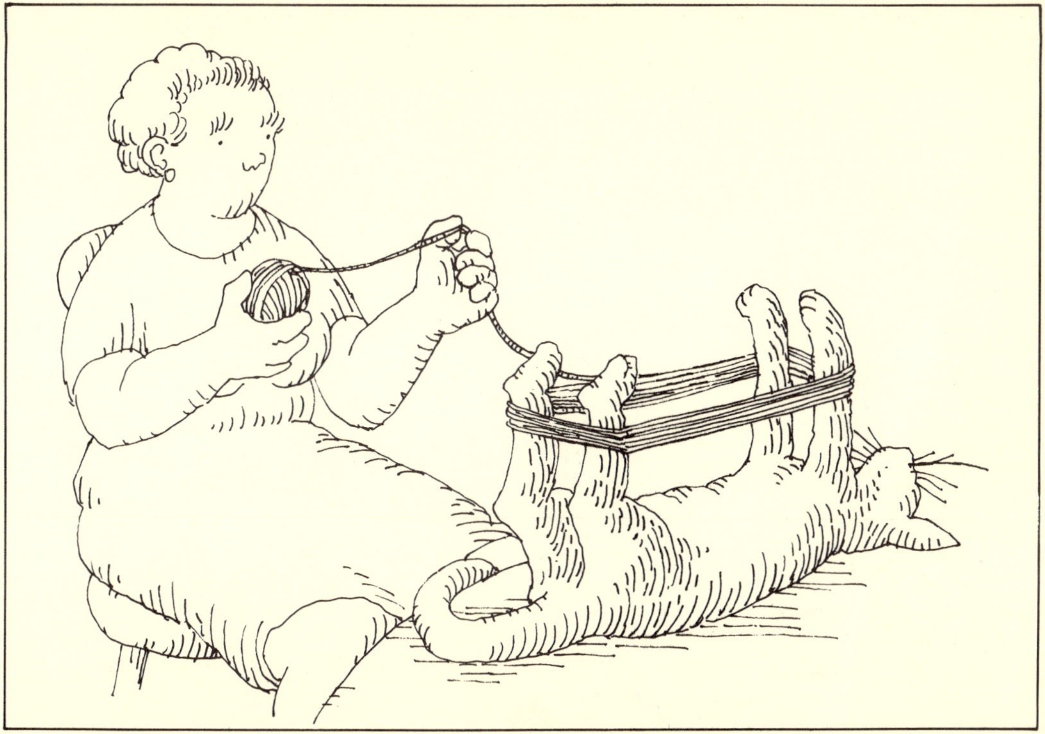

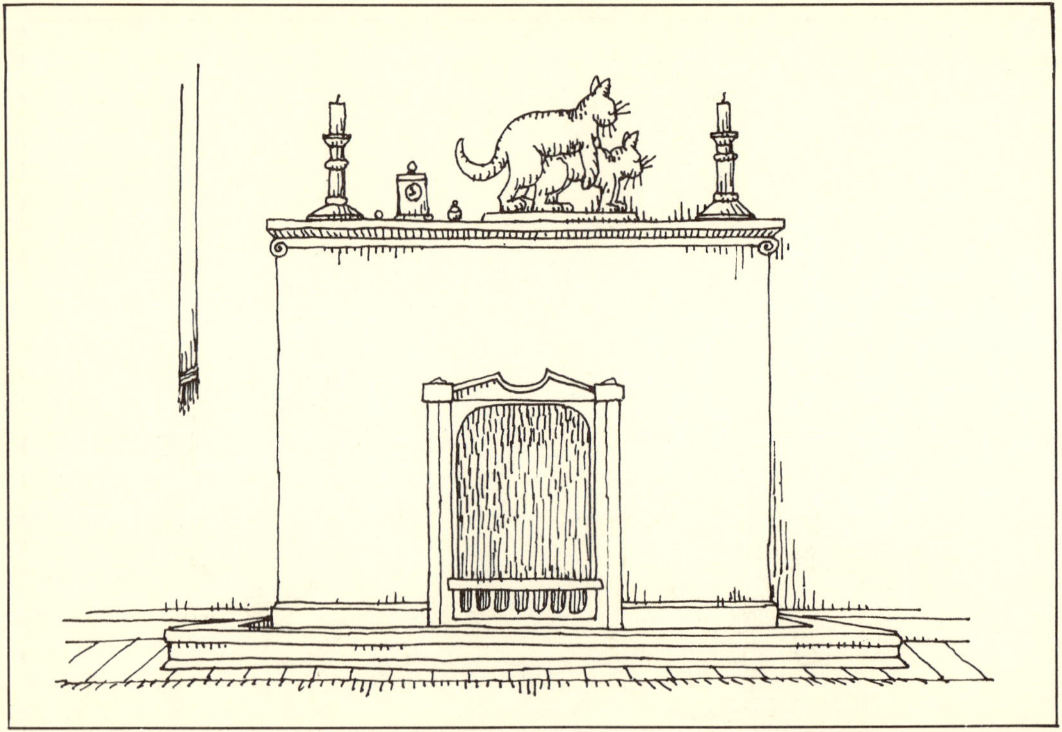

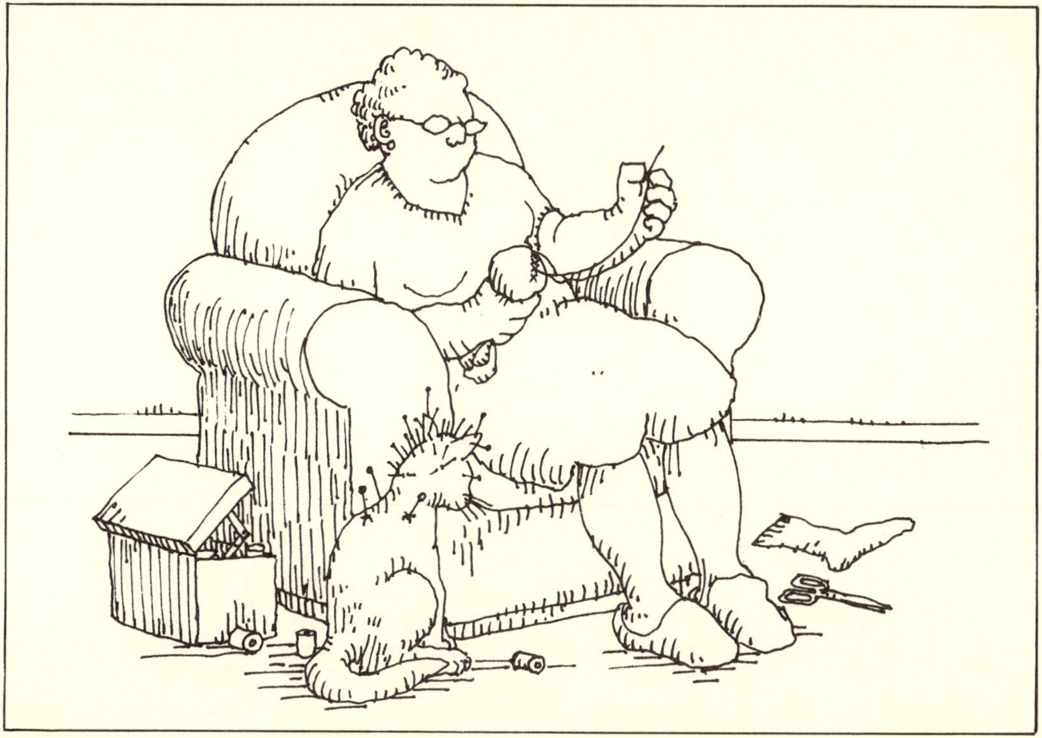

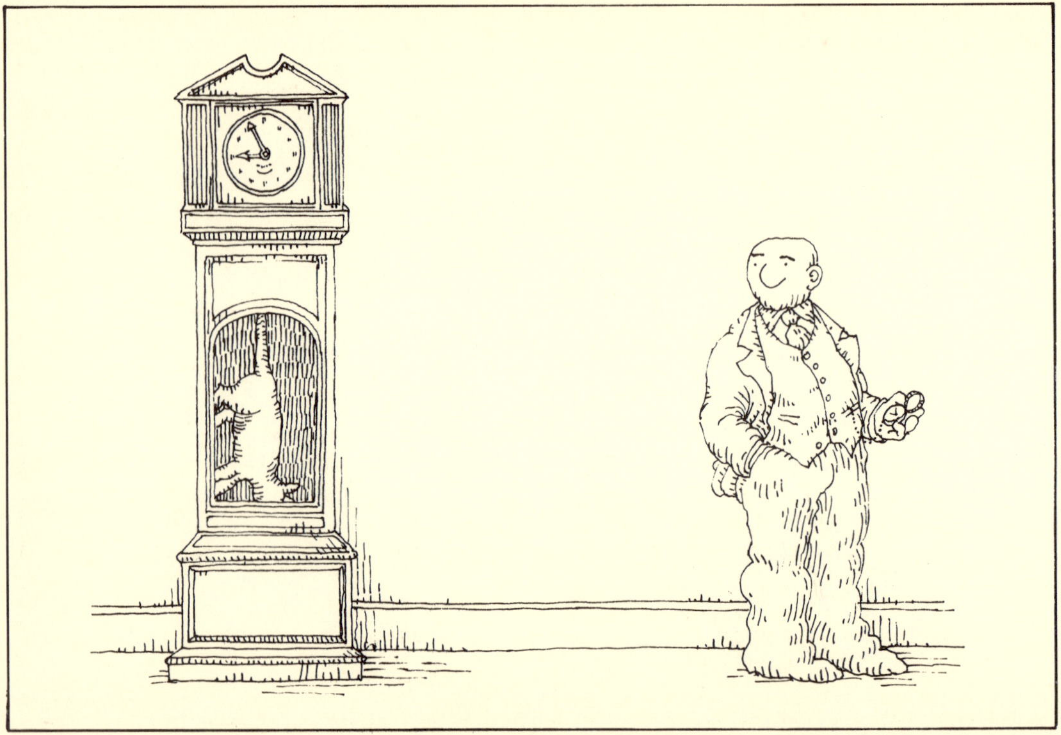

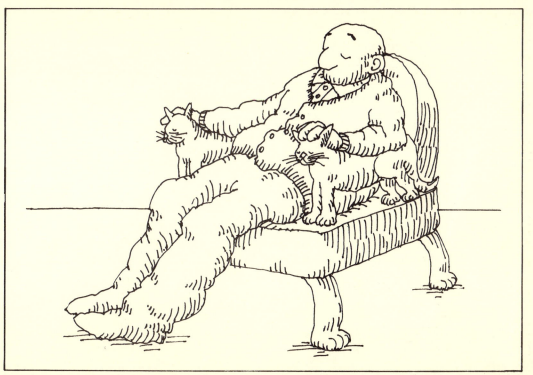

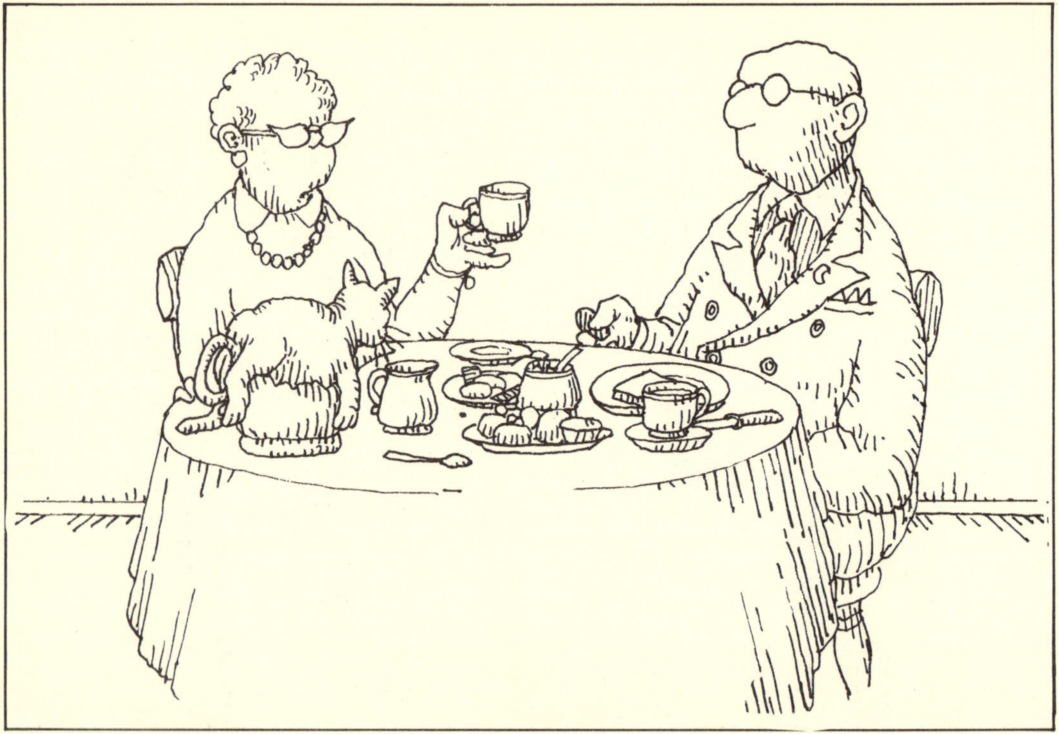

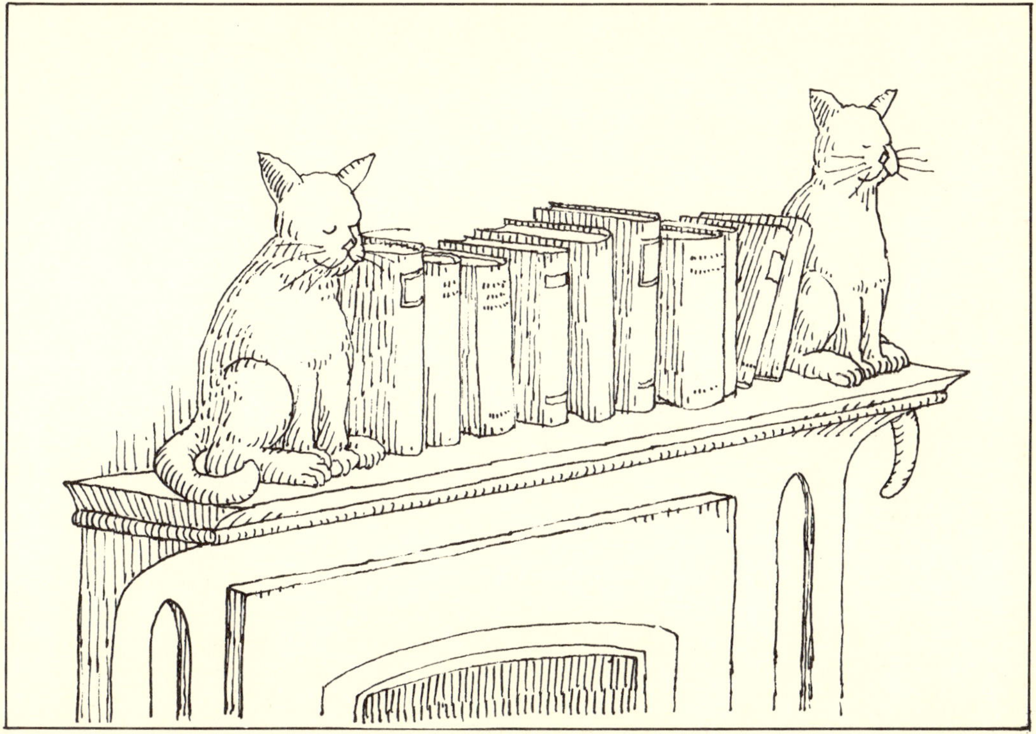

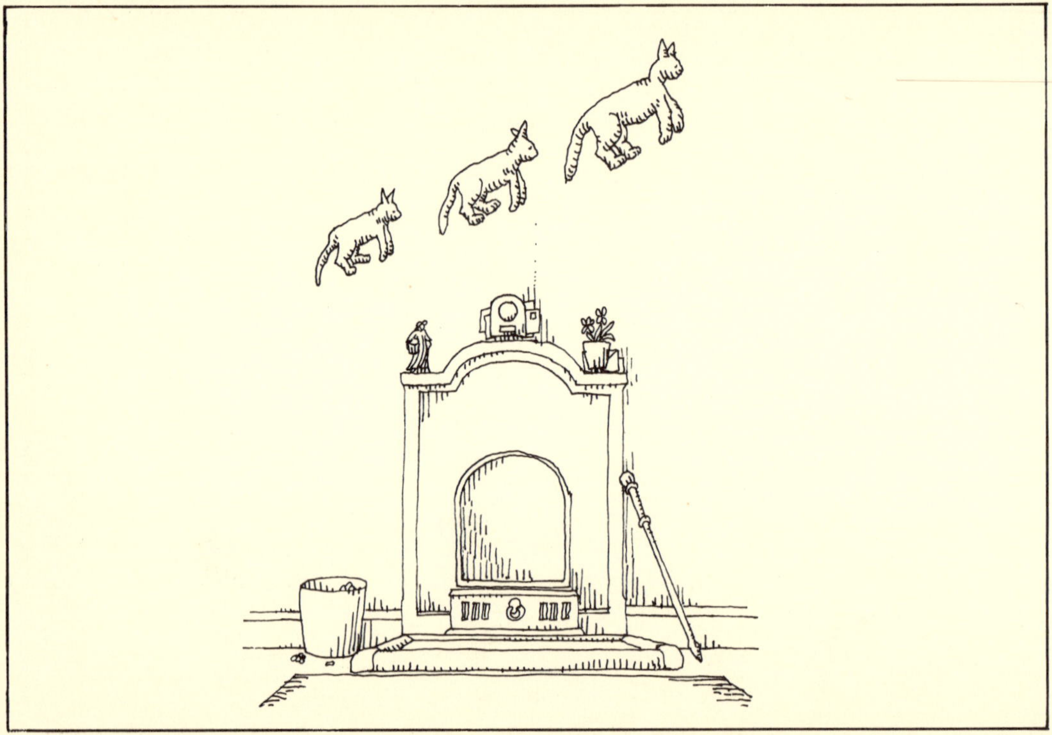

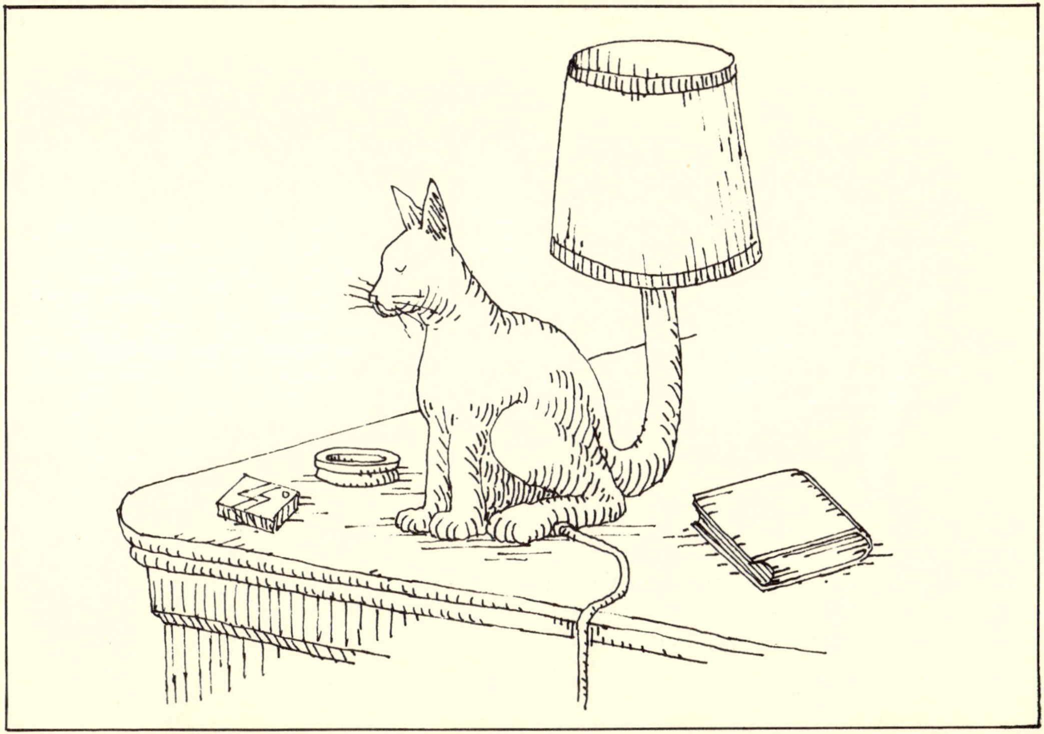

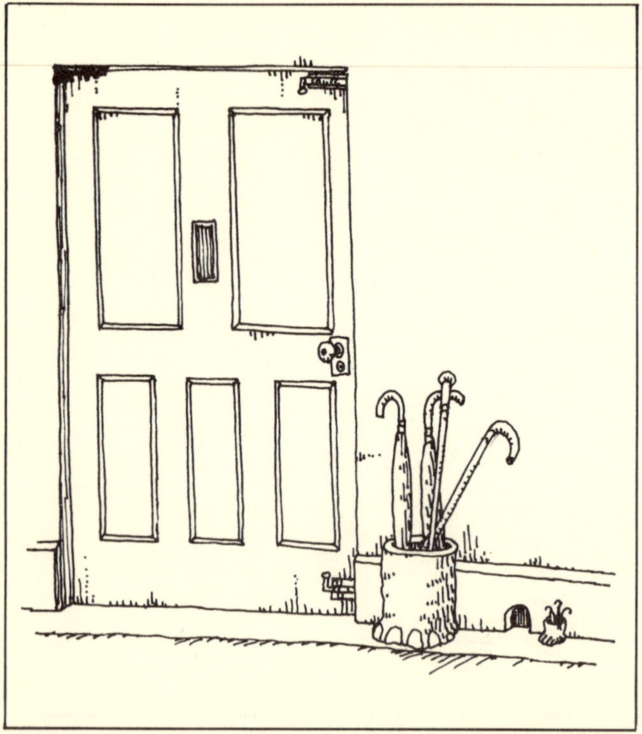

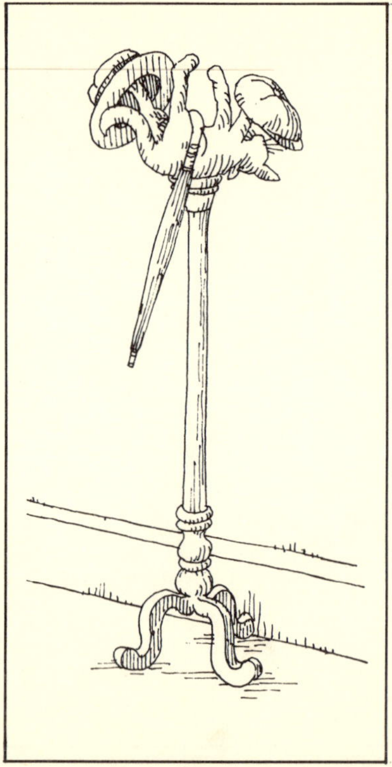

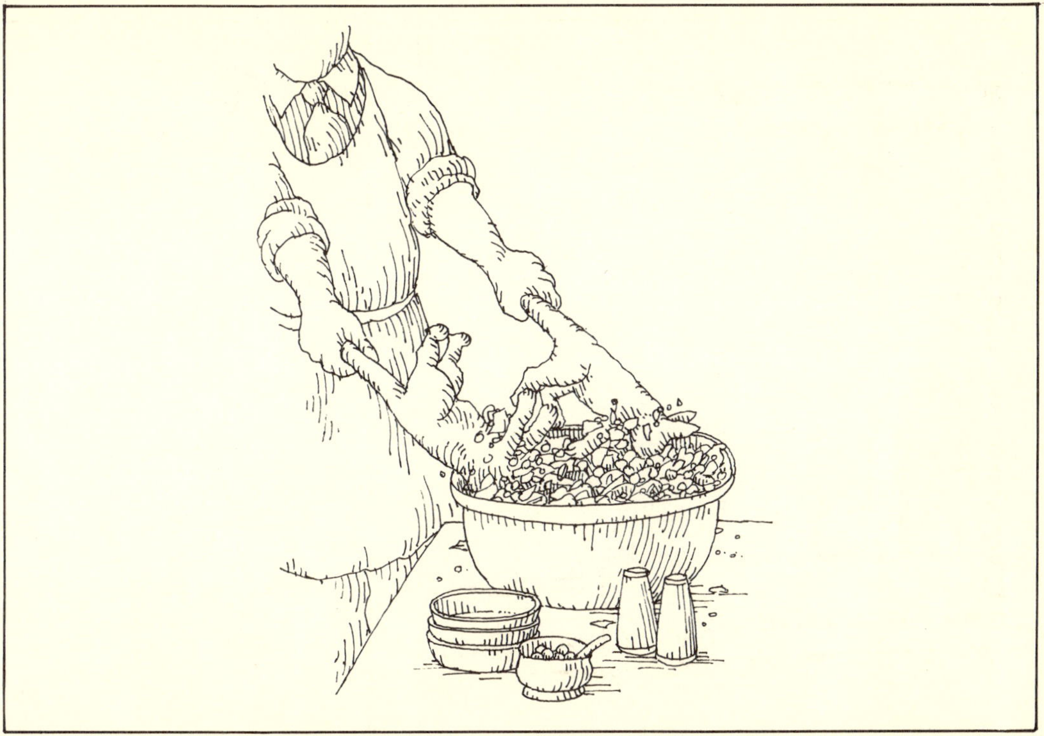

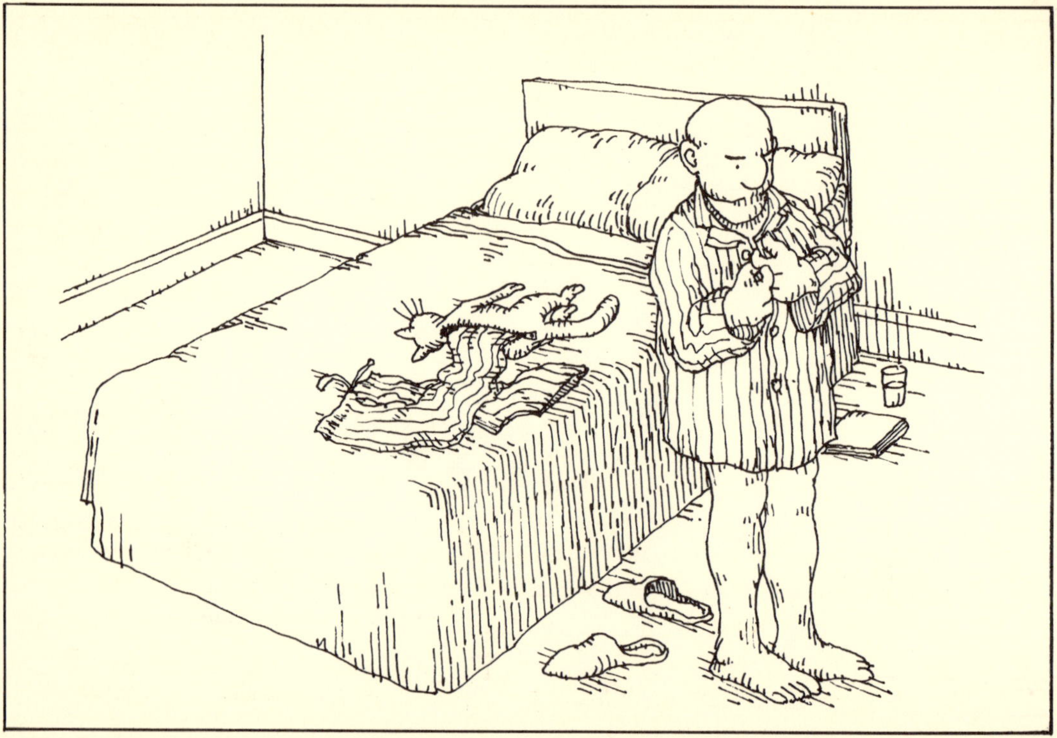

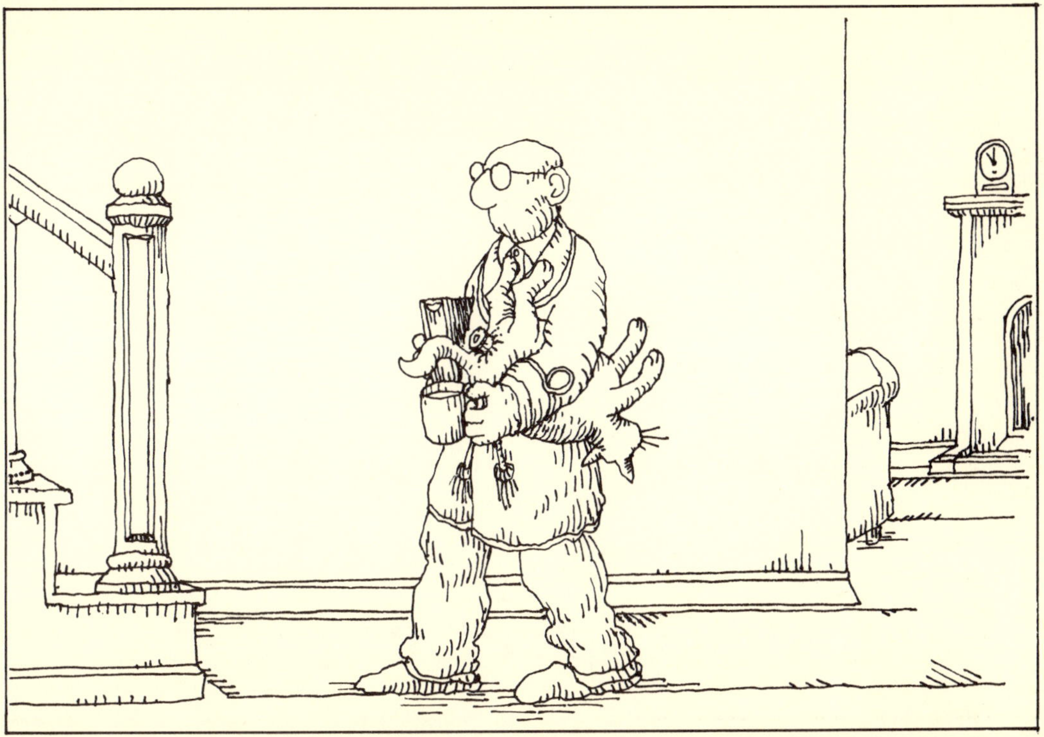

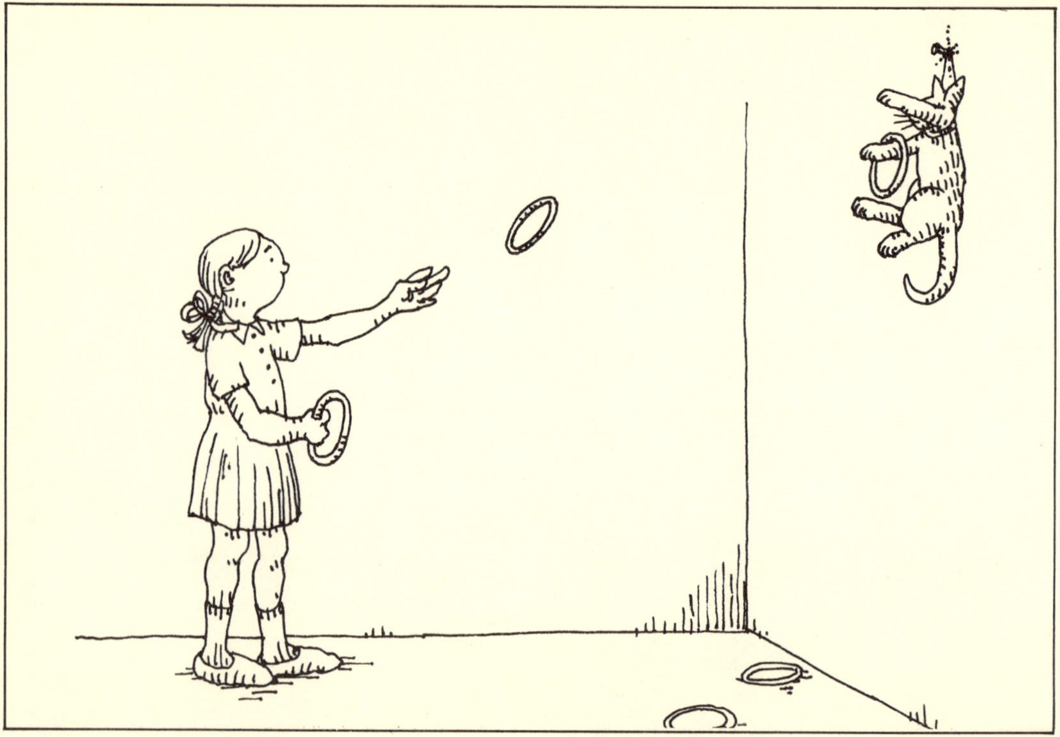

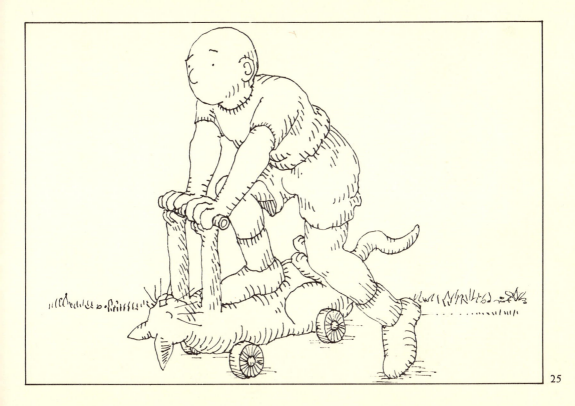

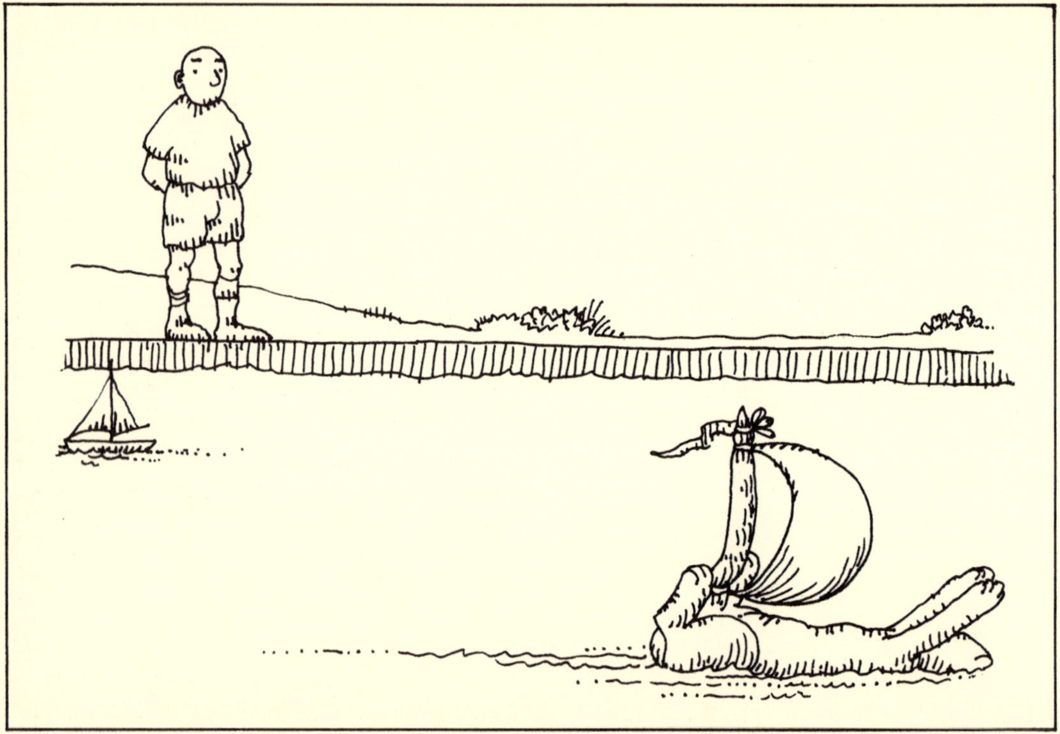

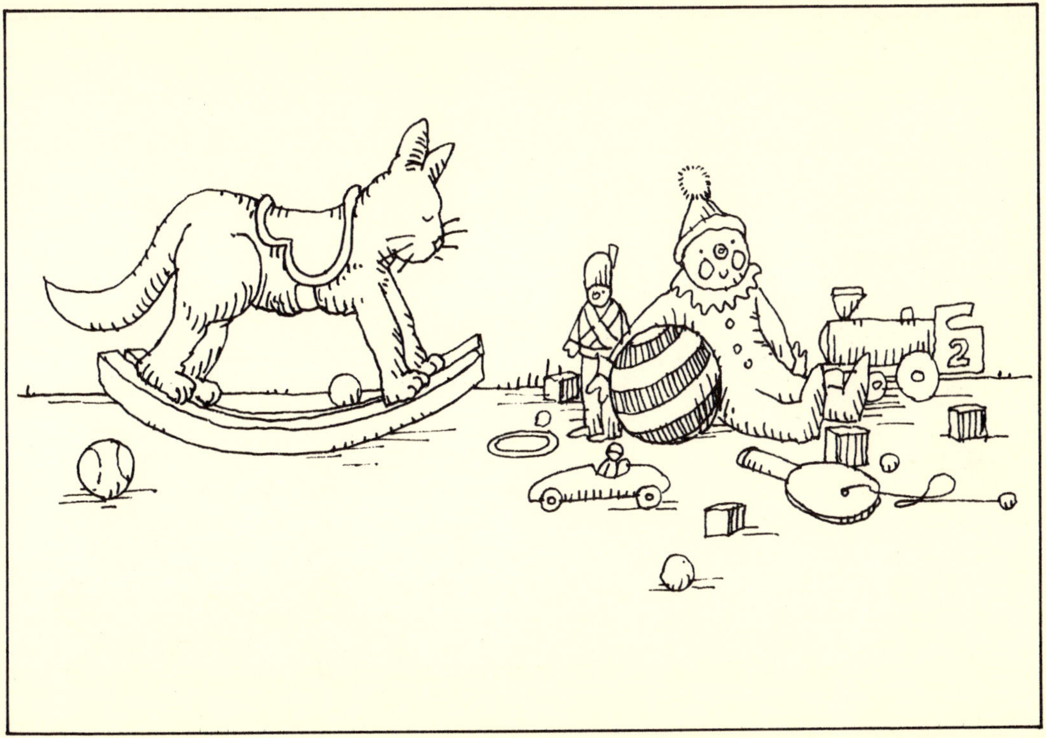
2

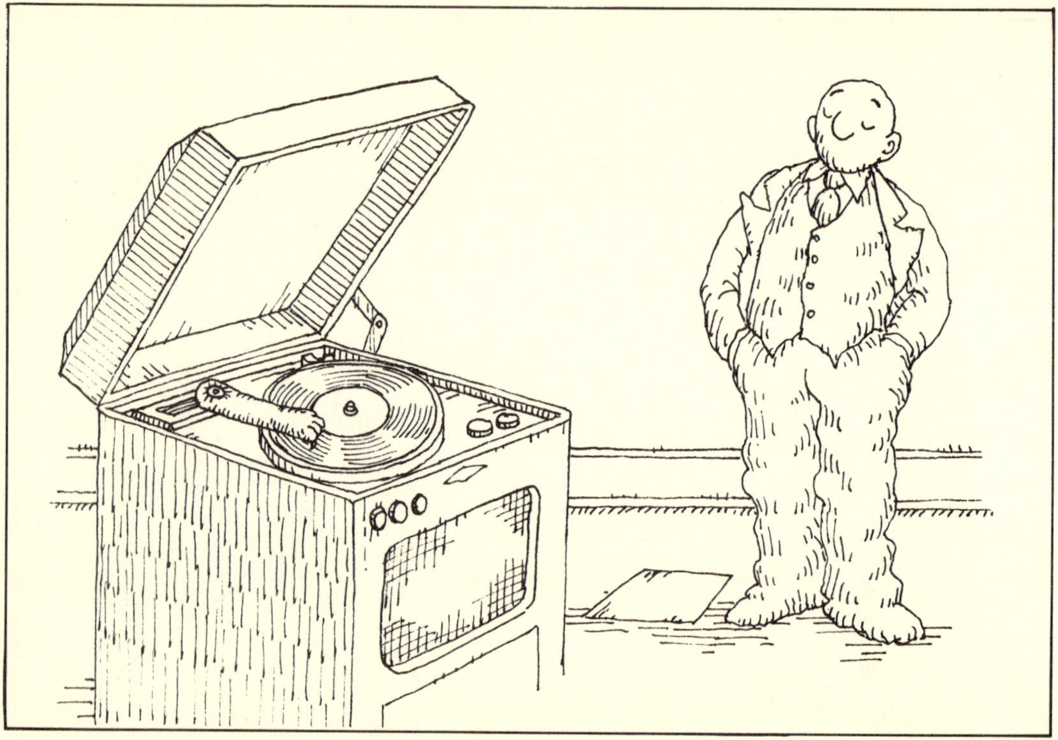

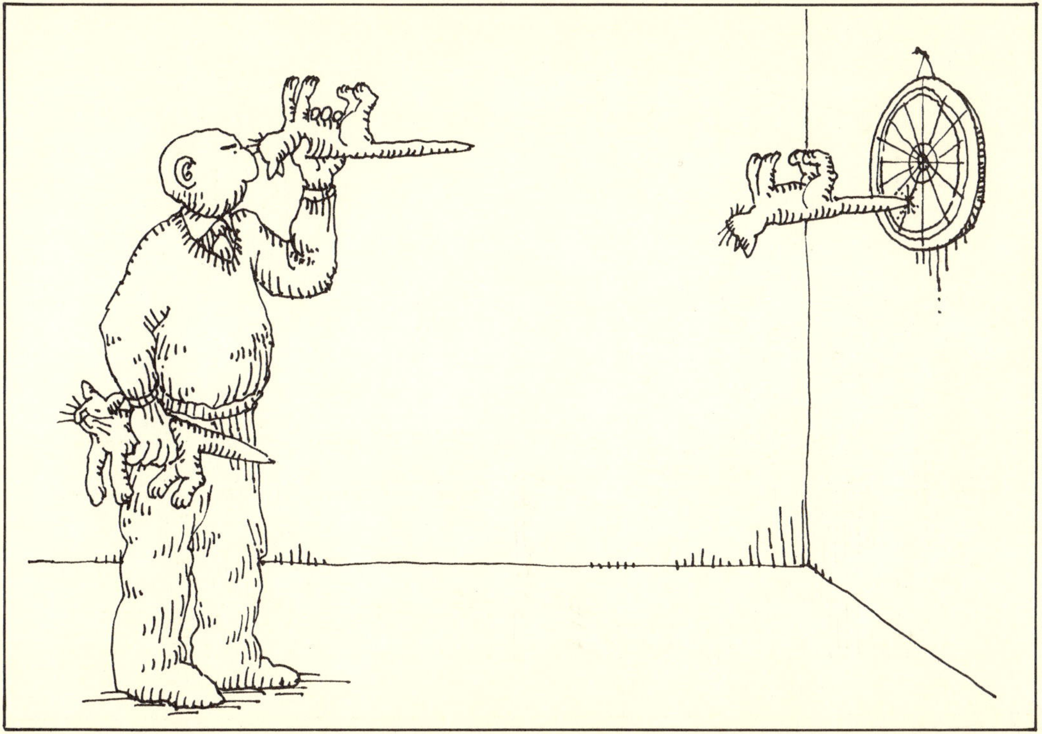

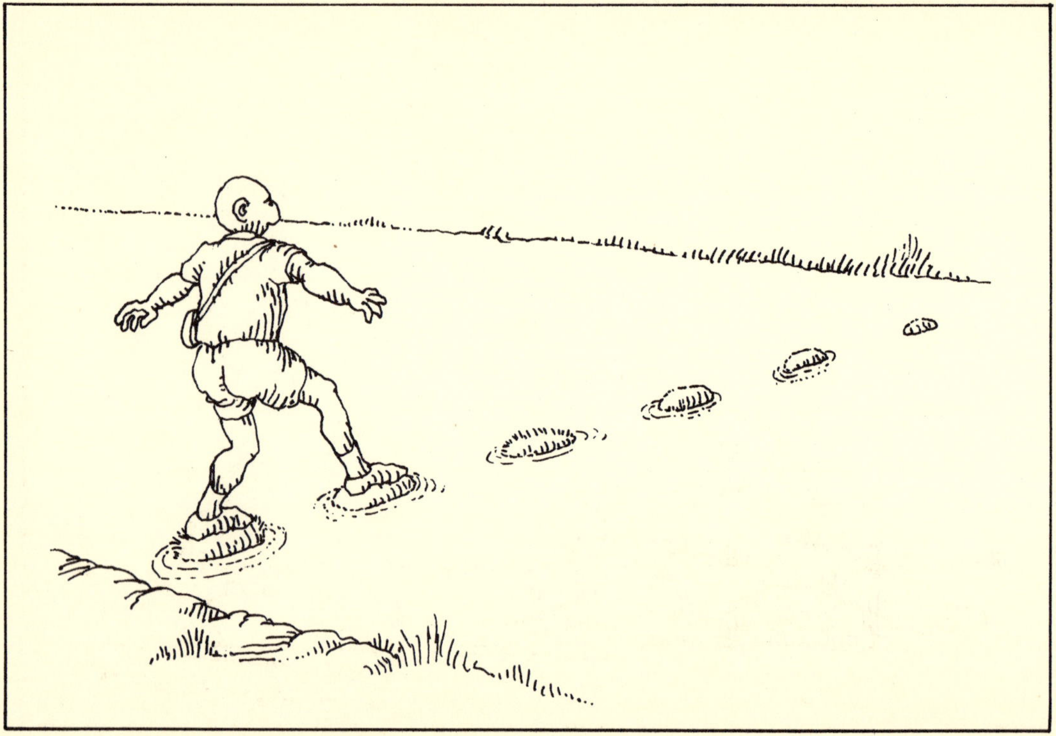

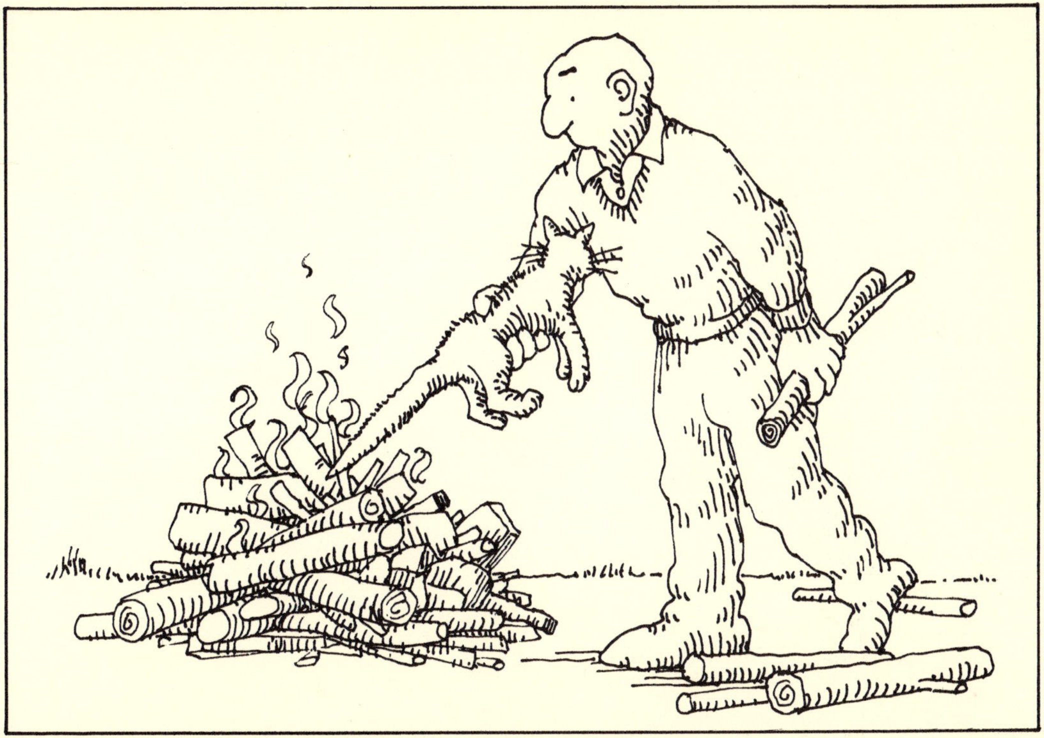

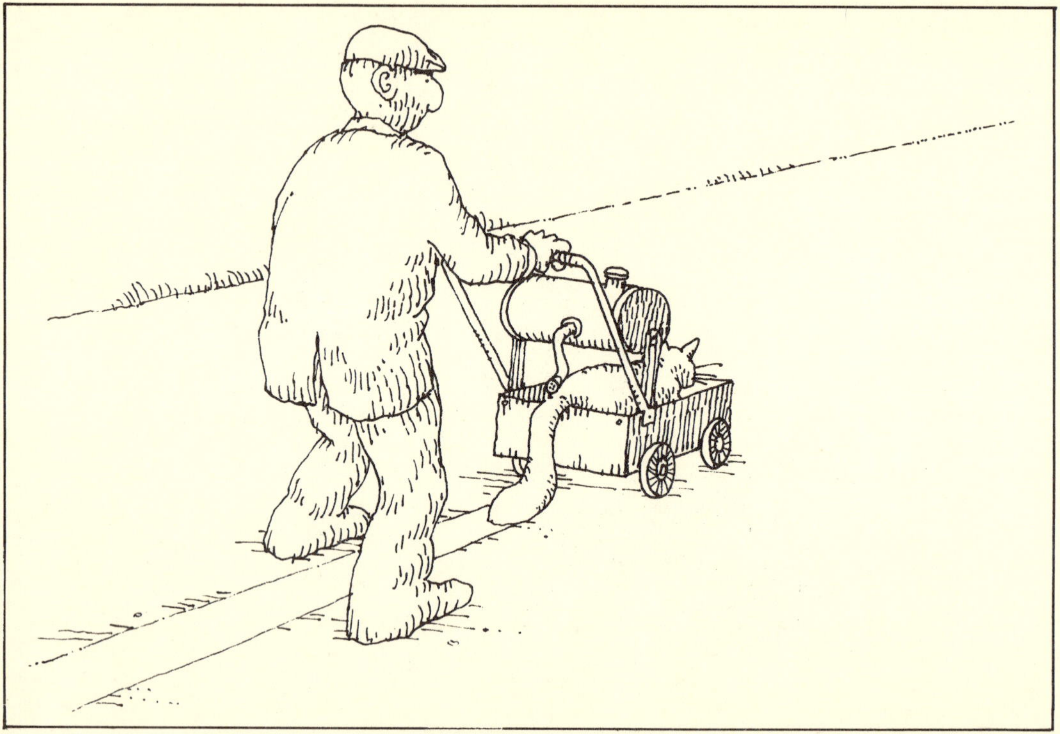

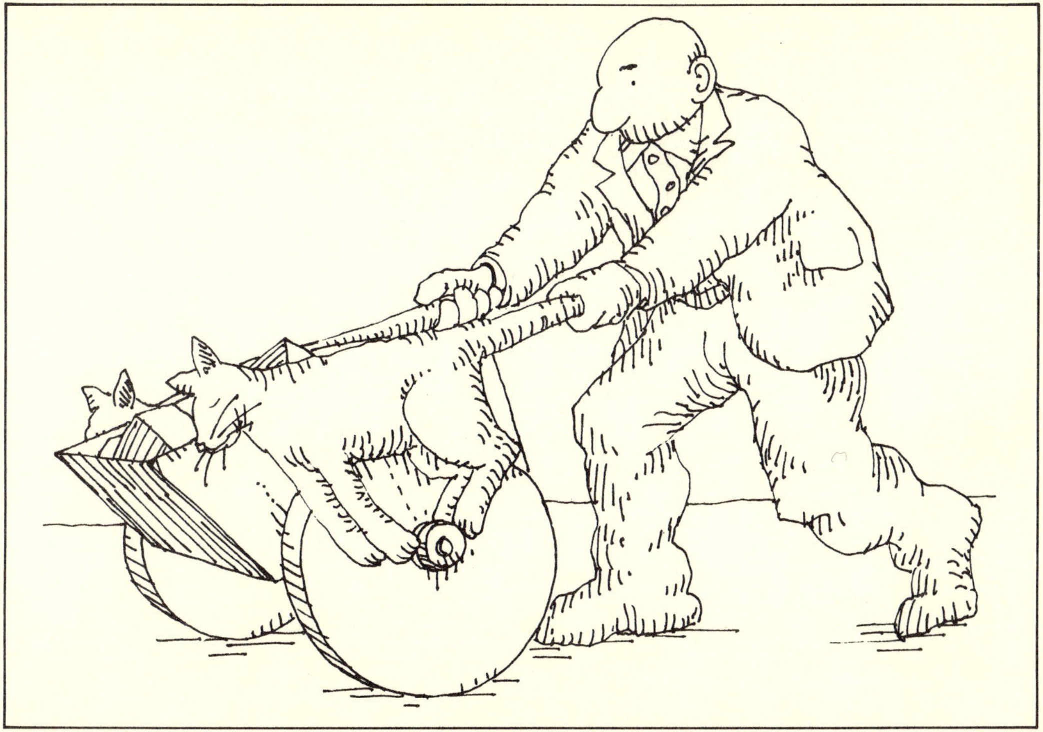

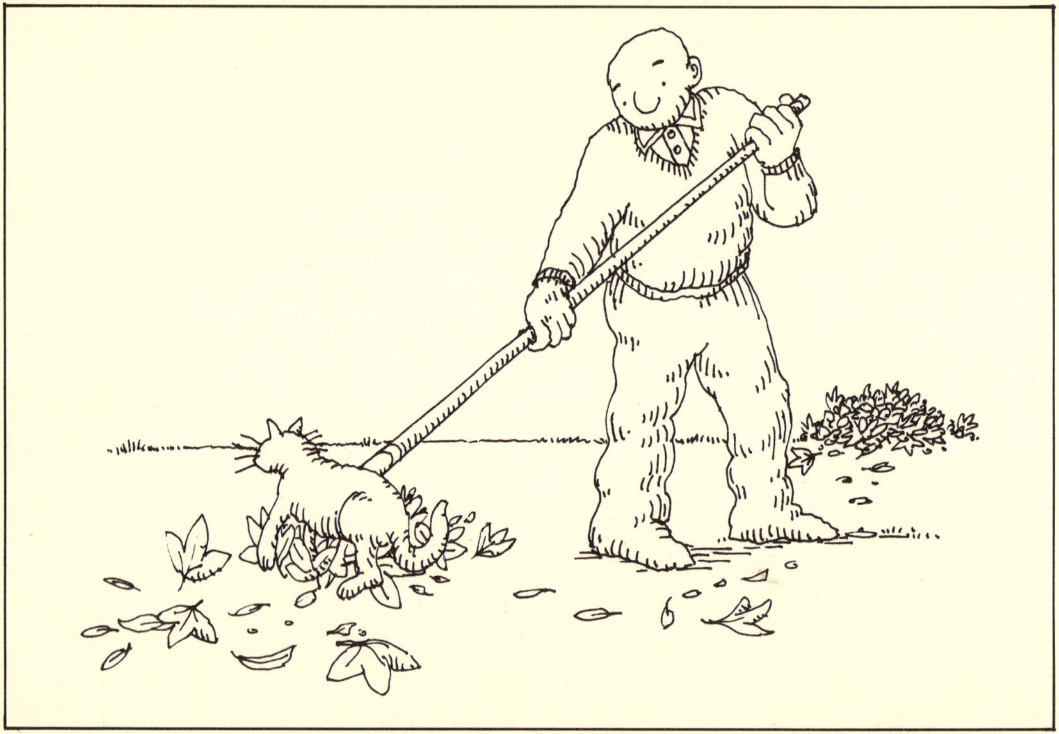

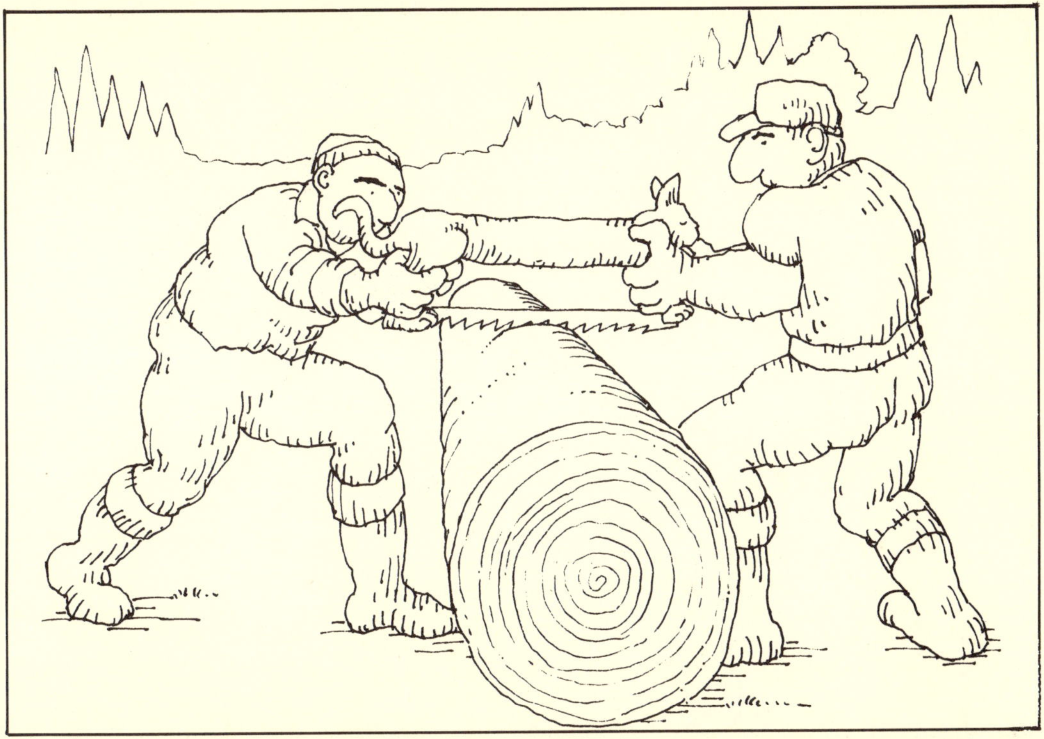

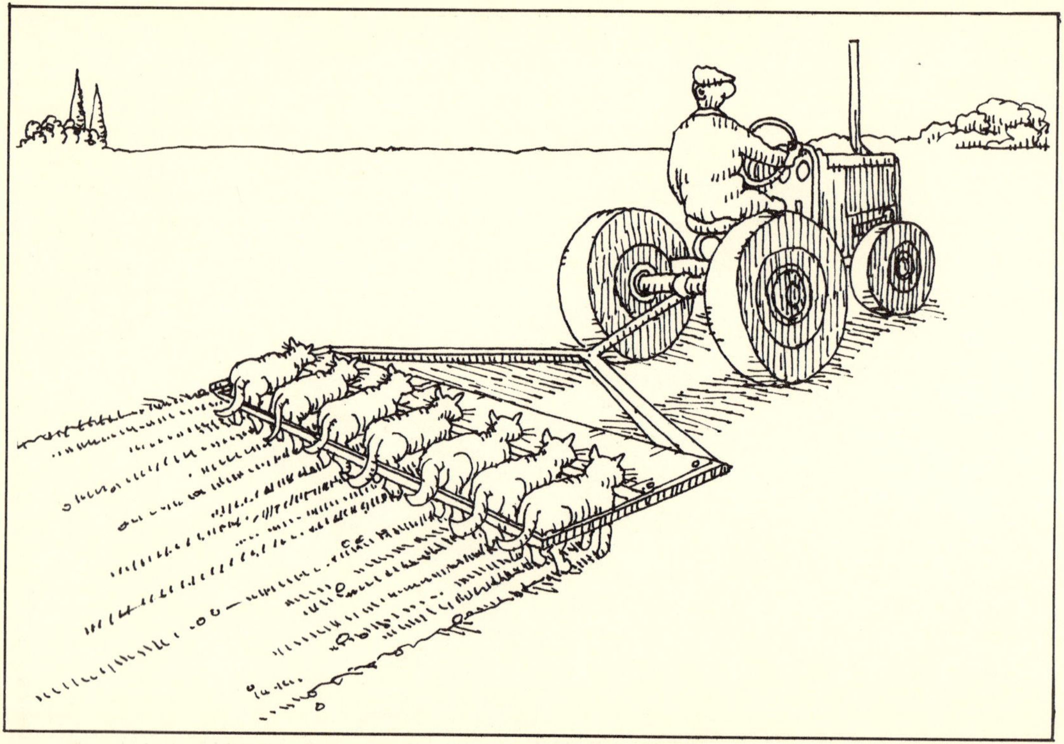

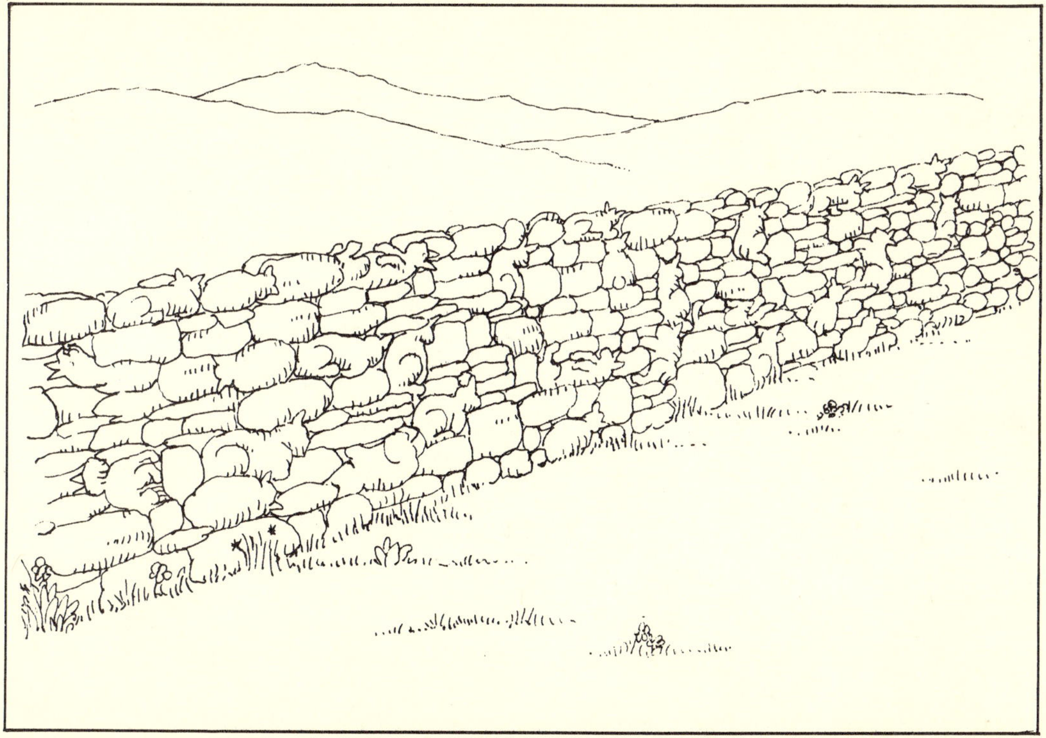

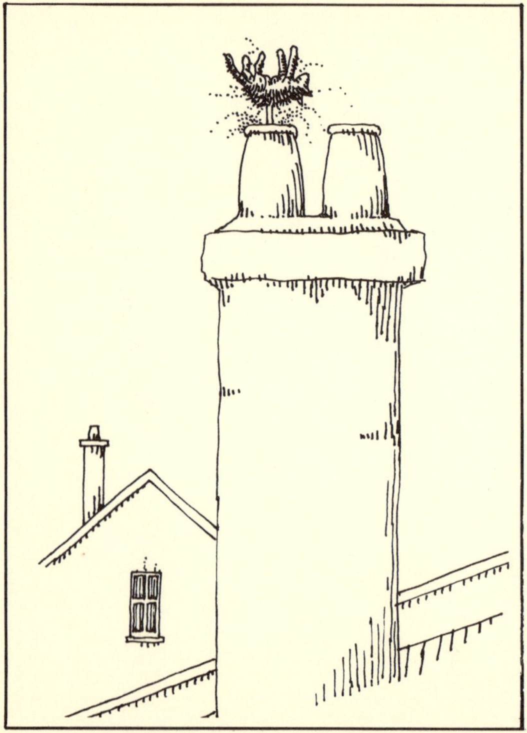

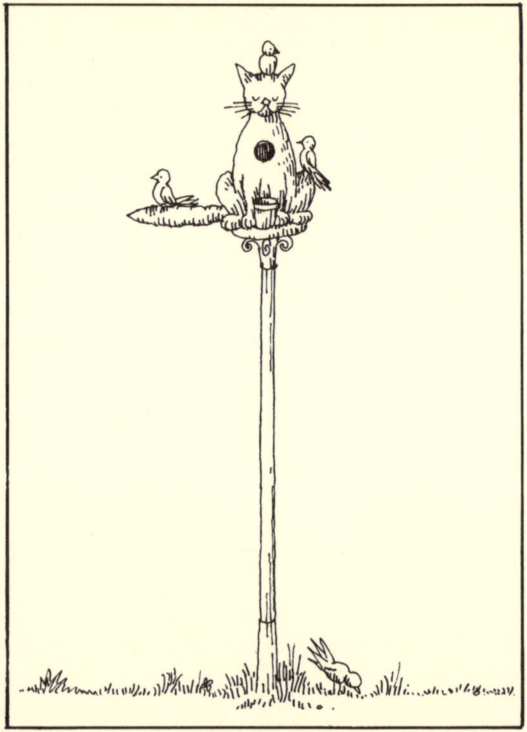

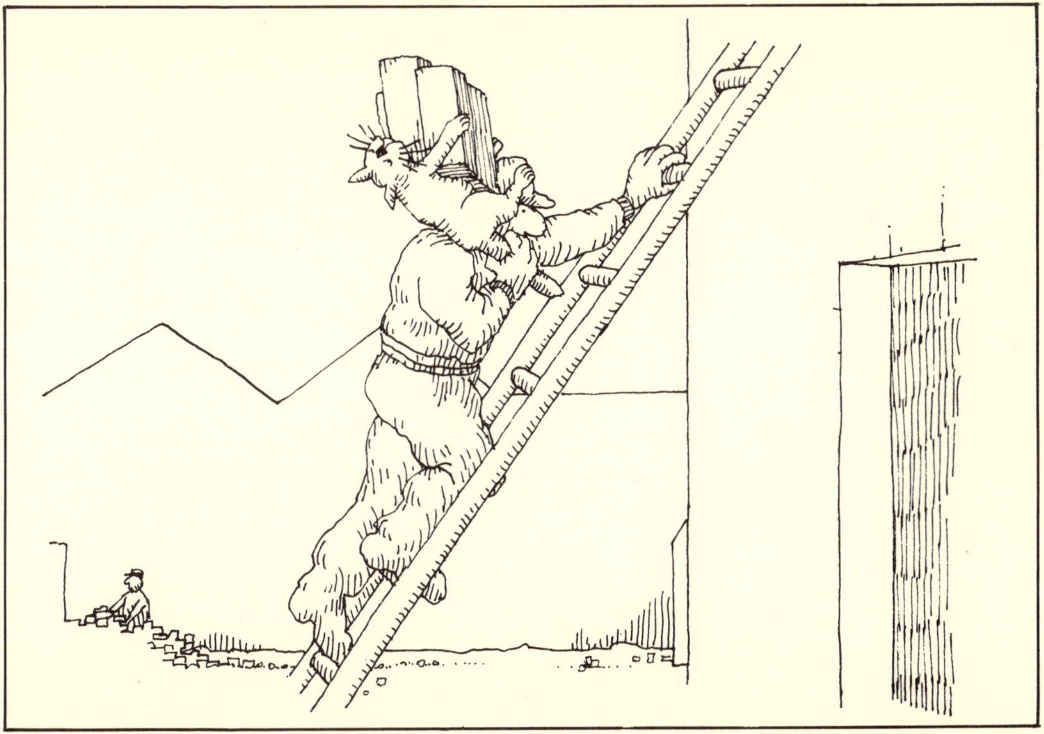

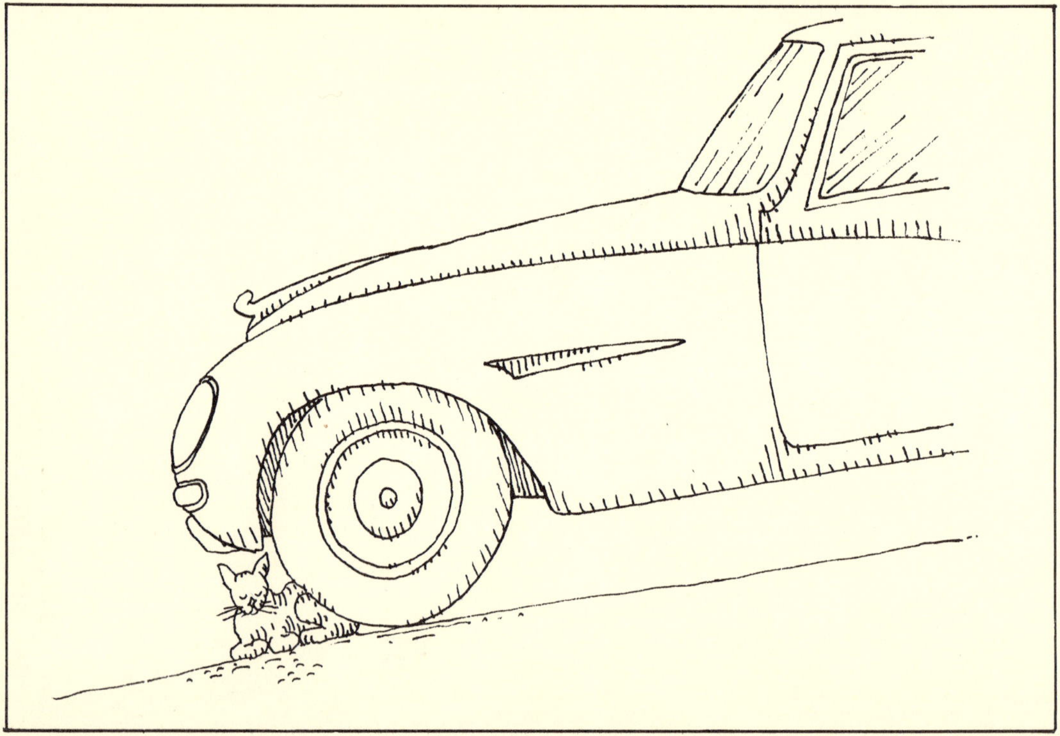

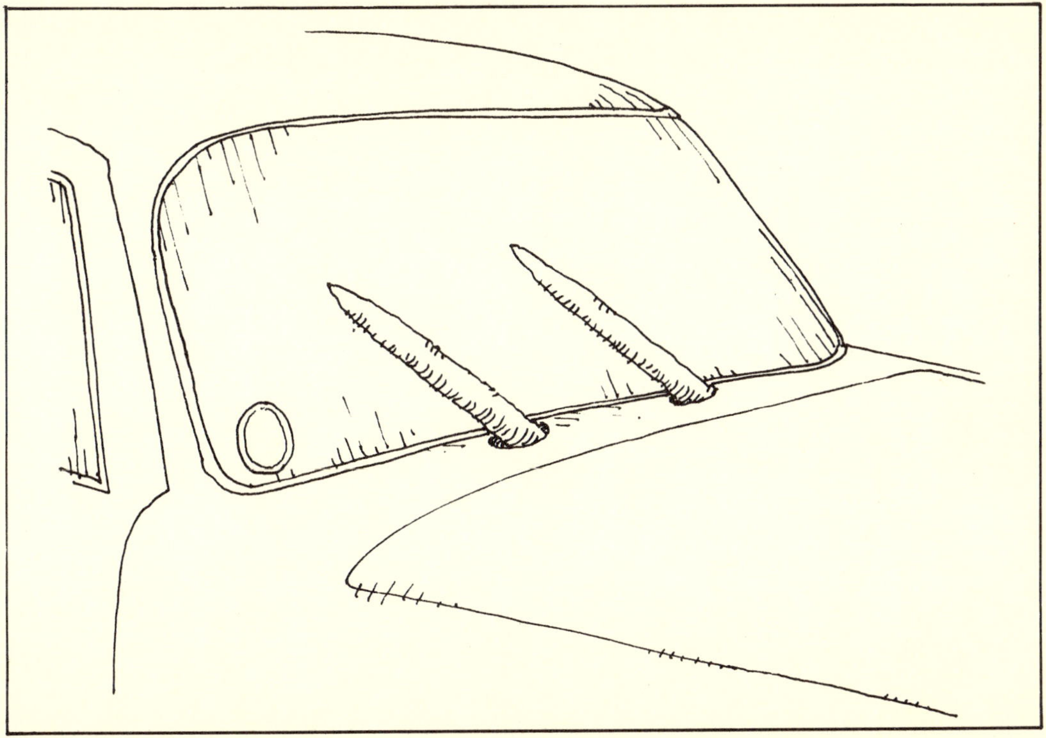

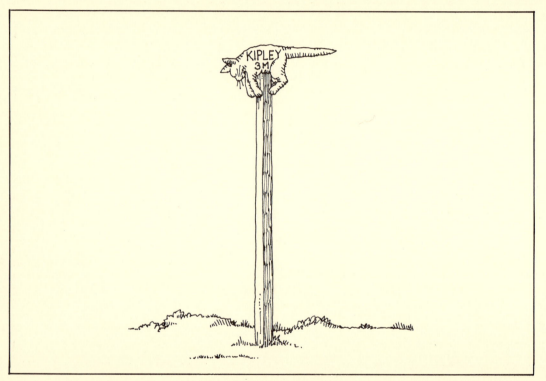

KIPLEY
3M

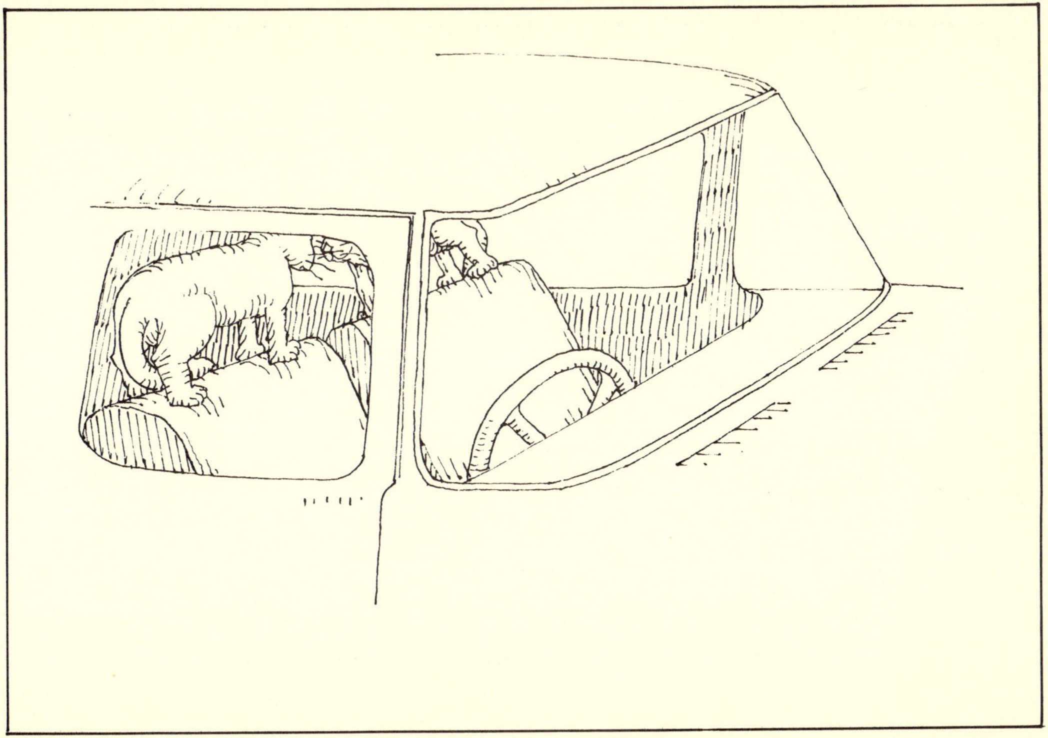

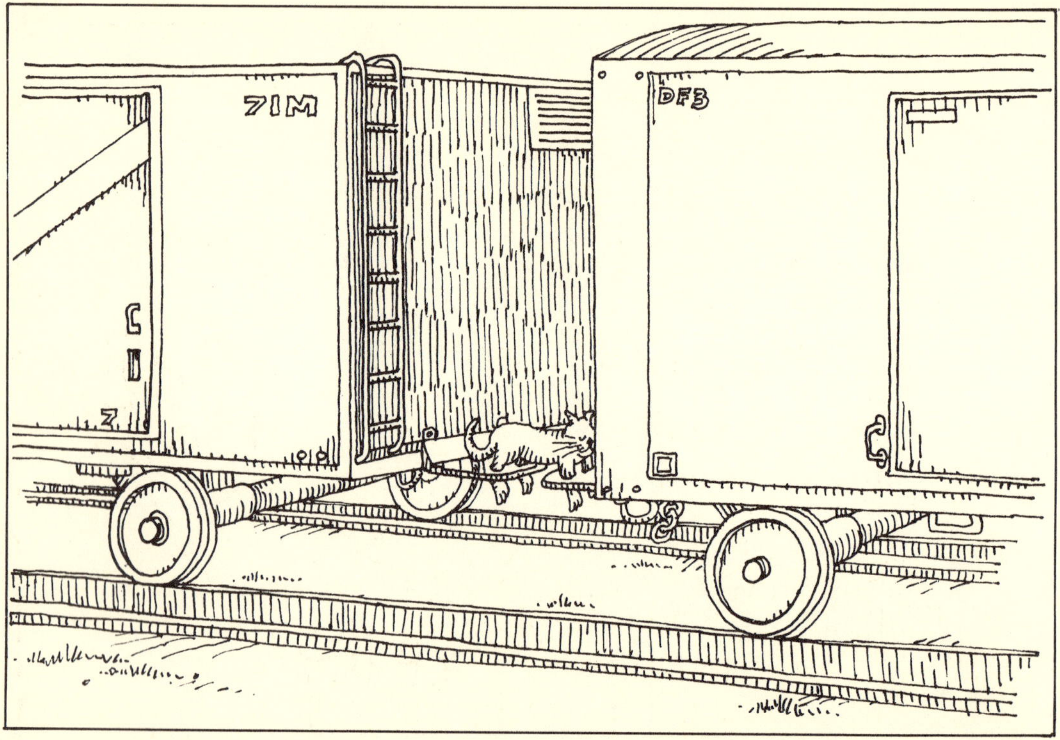
71M
DF3

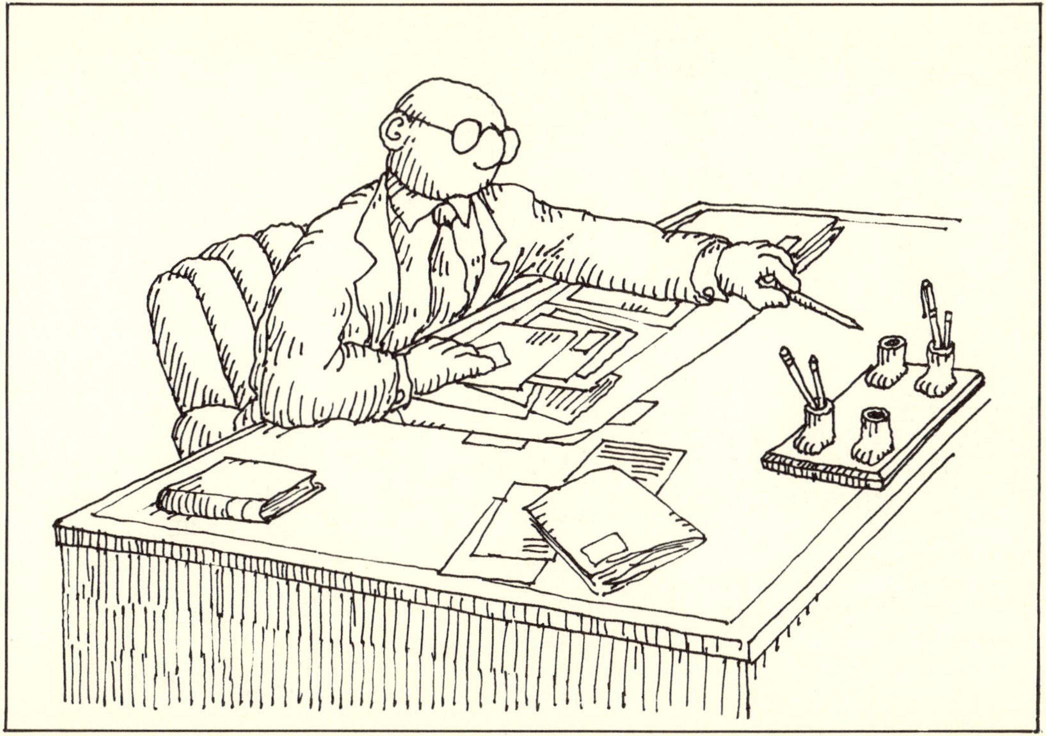

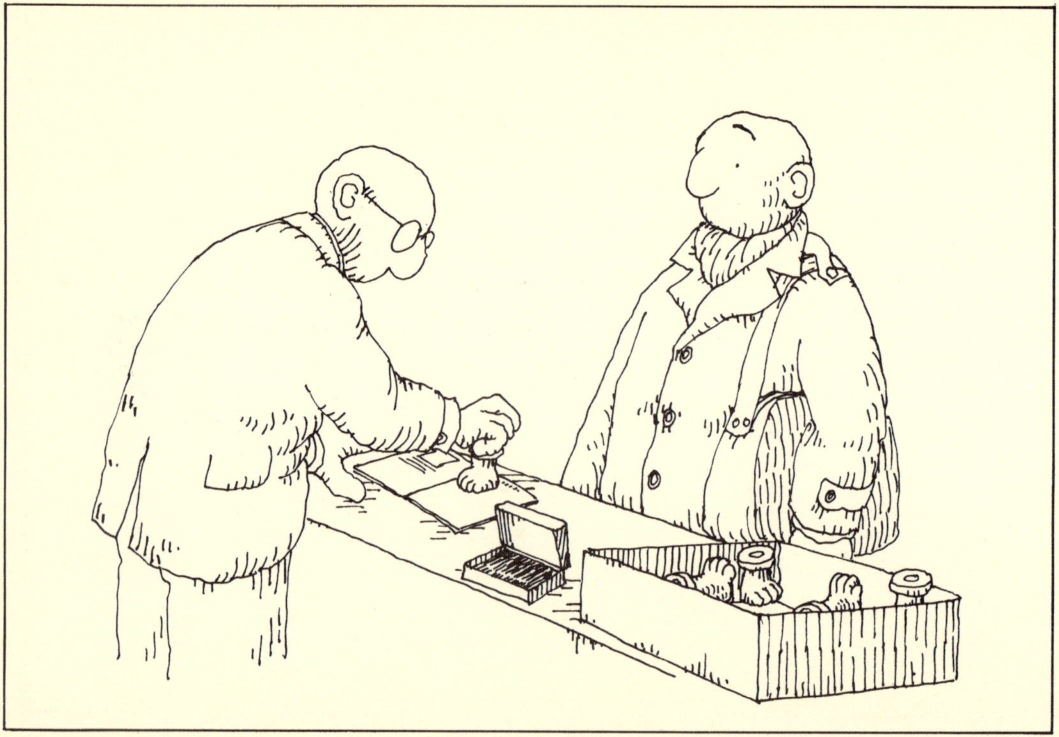

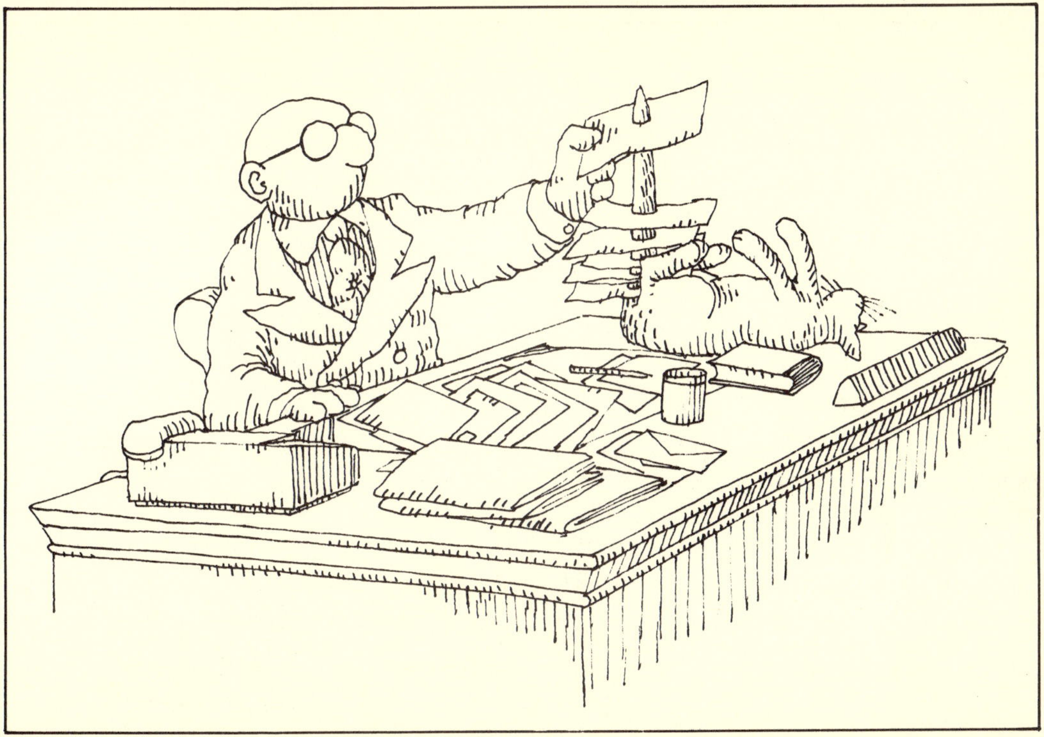

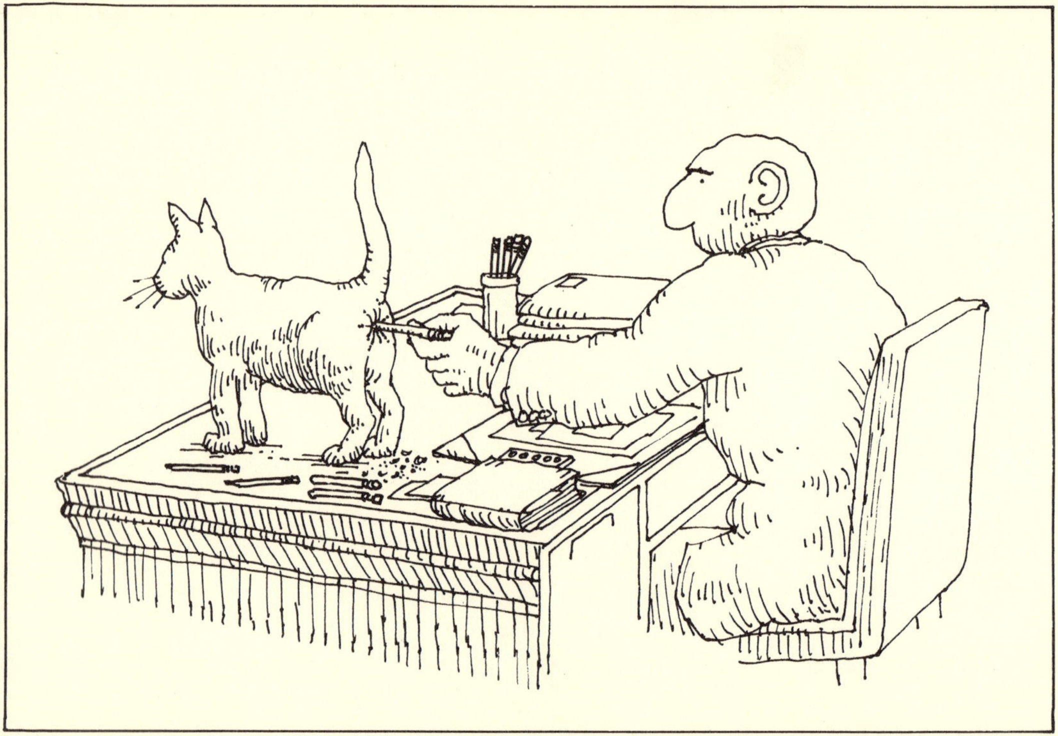

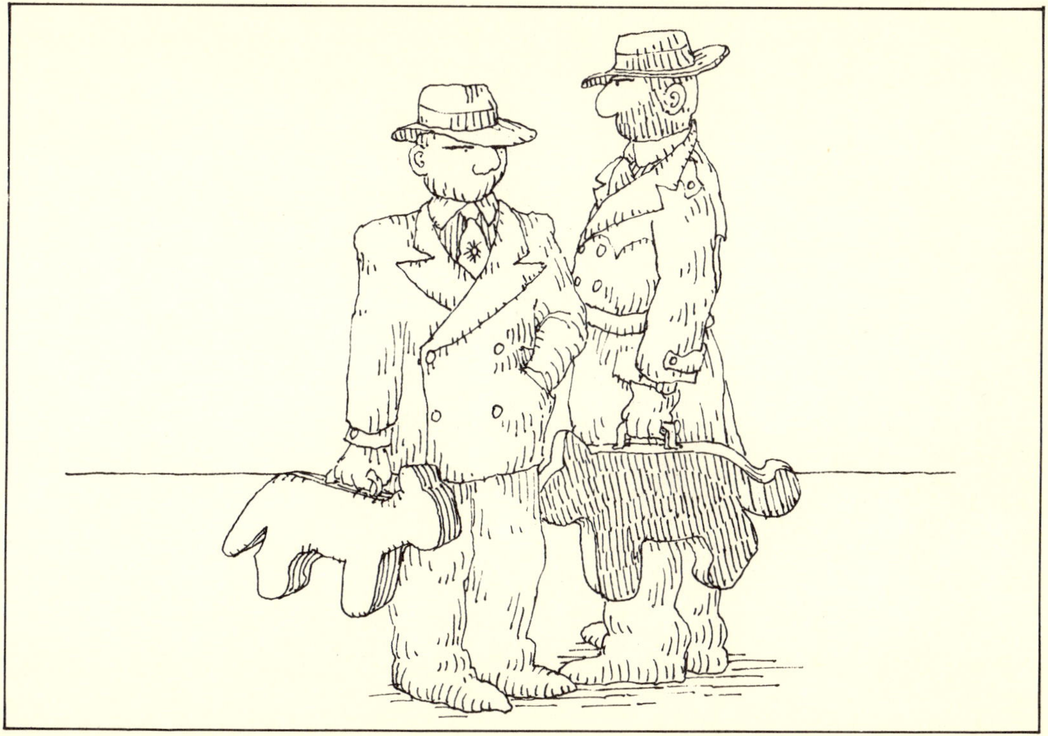

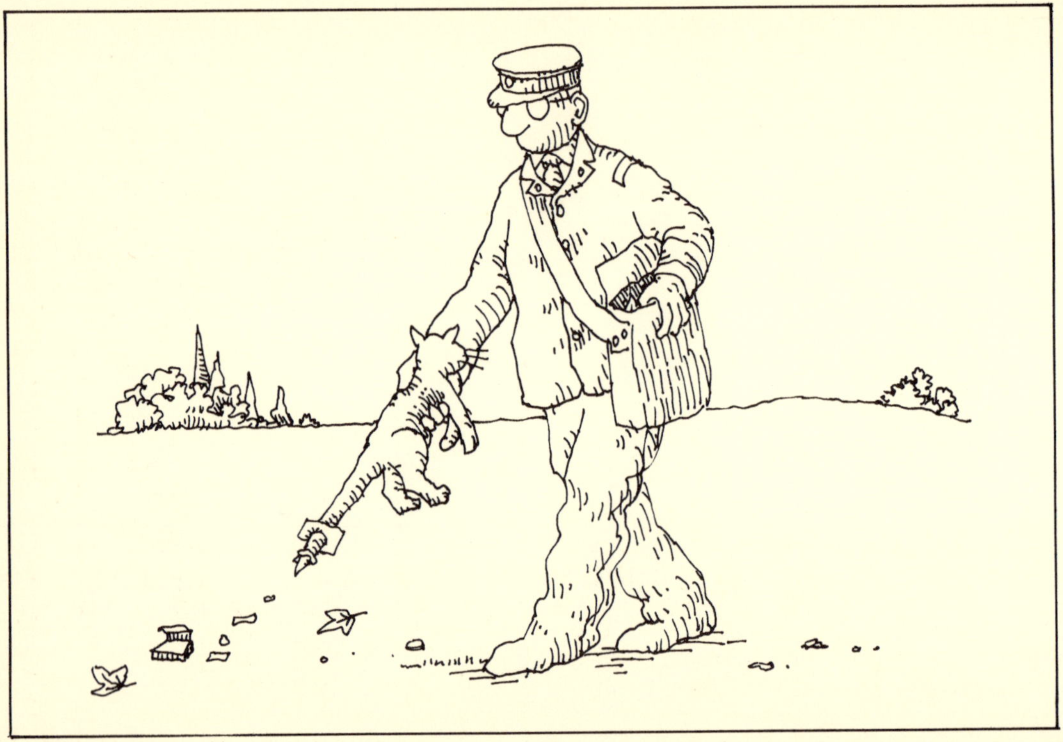

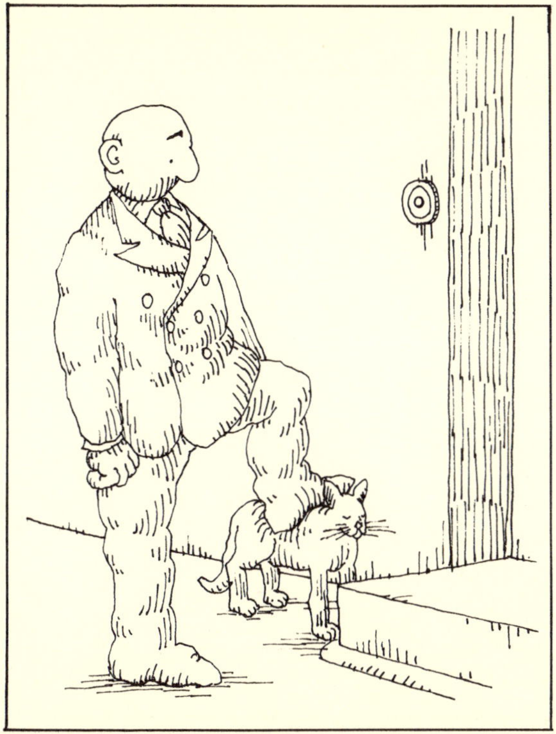

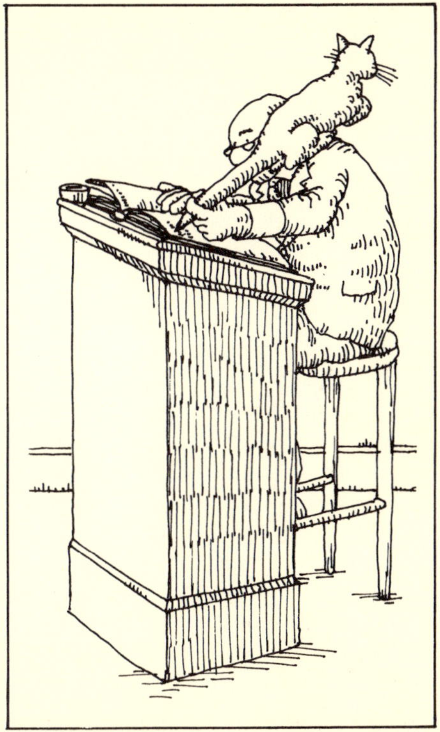

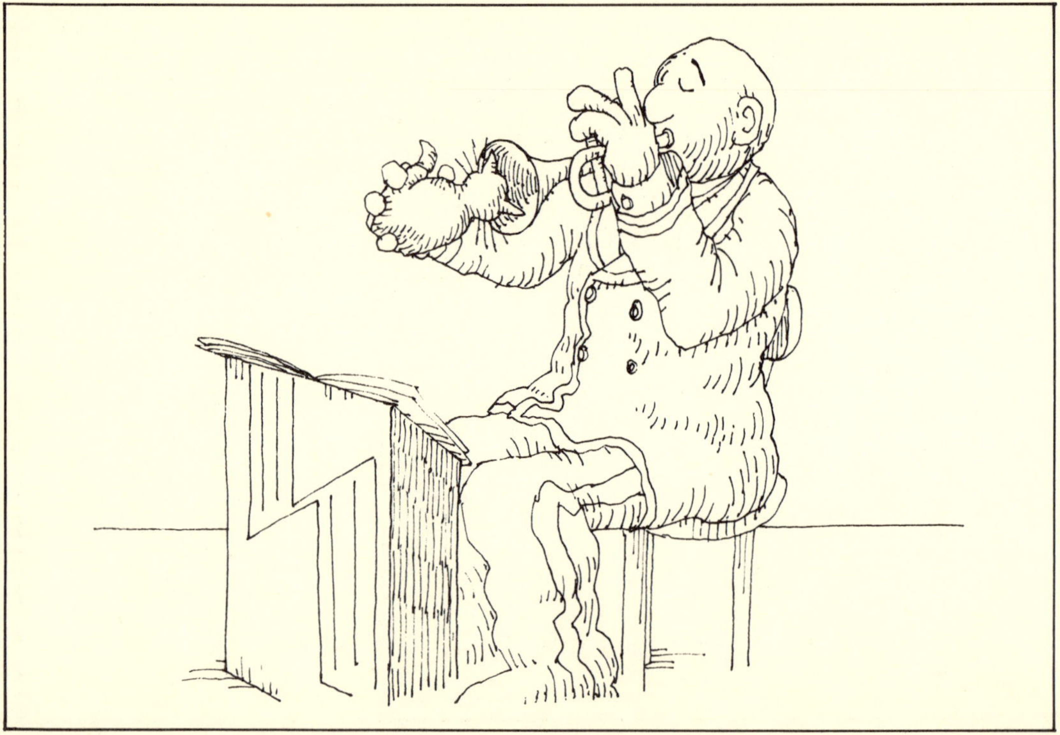

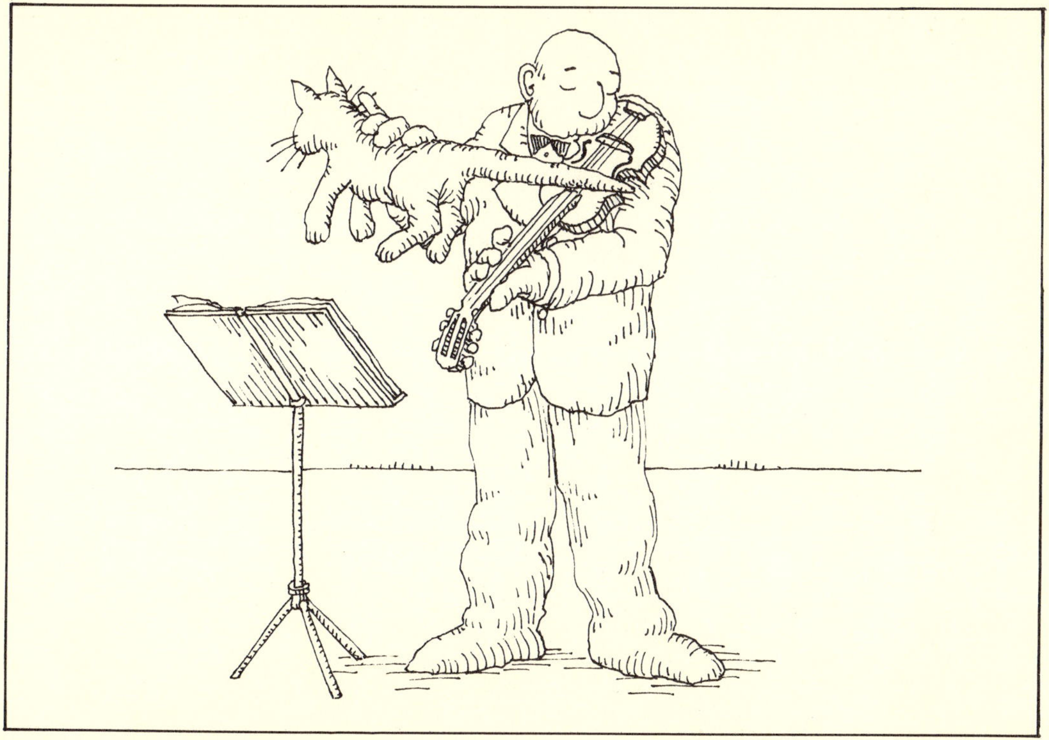

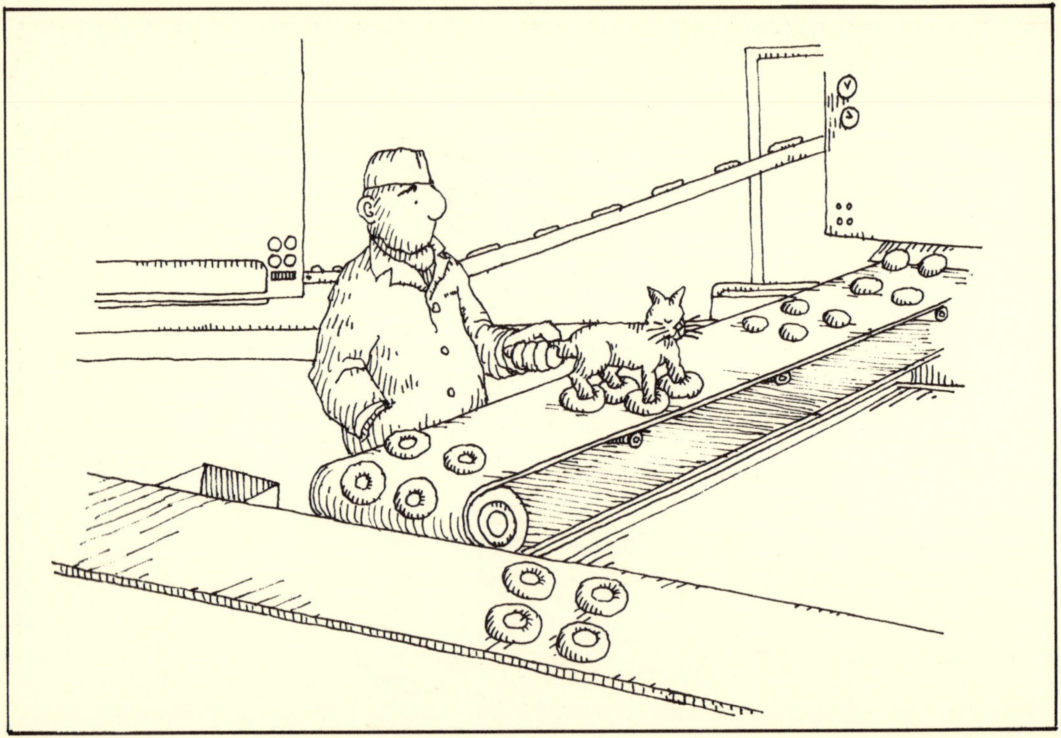

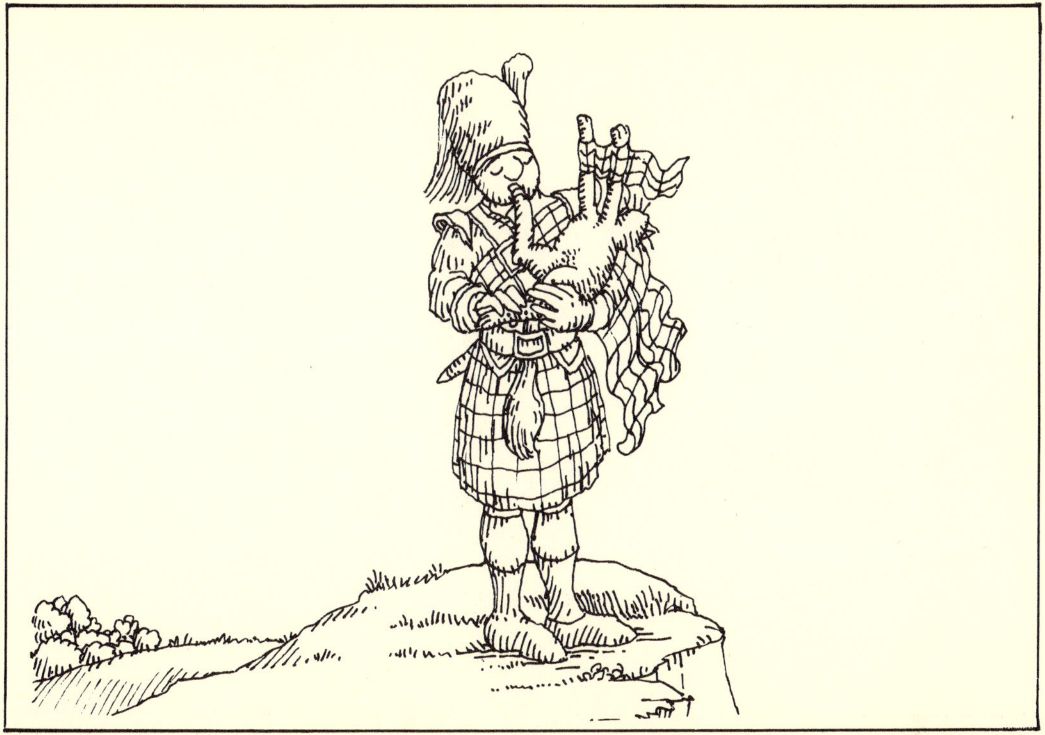

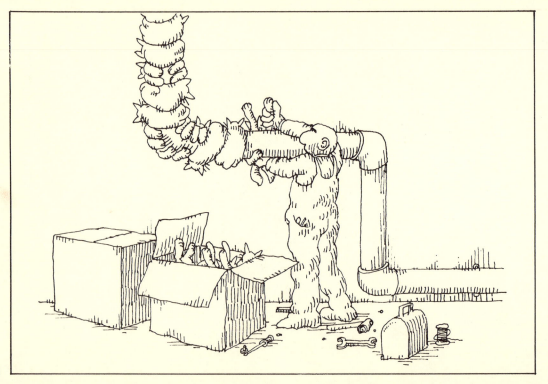

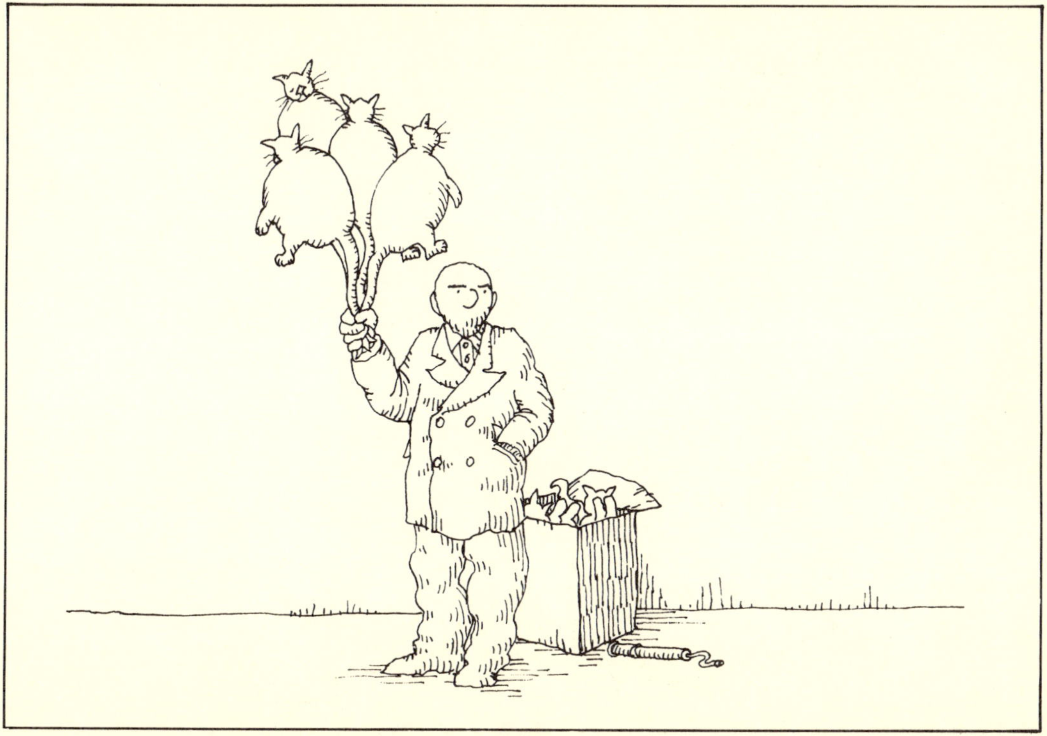

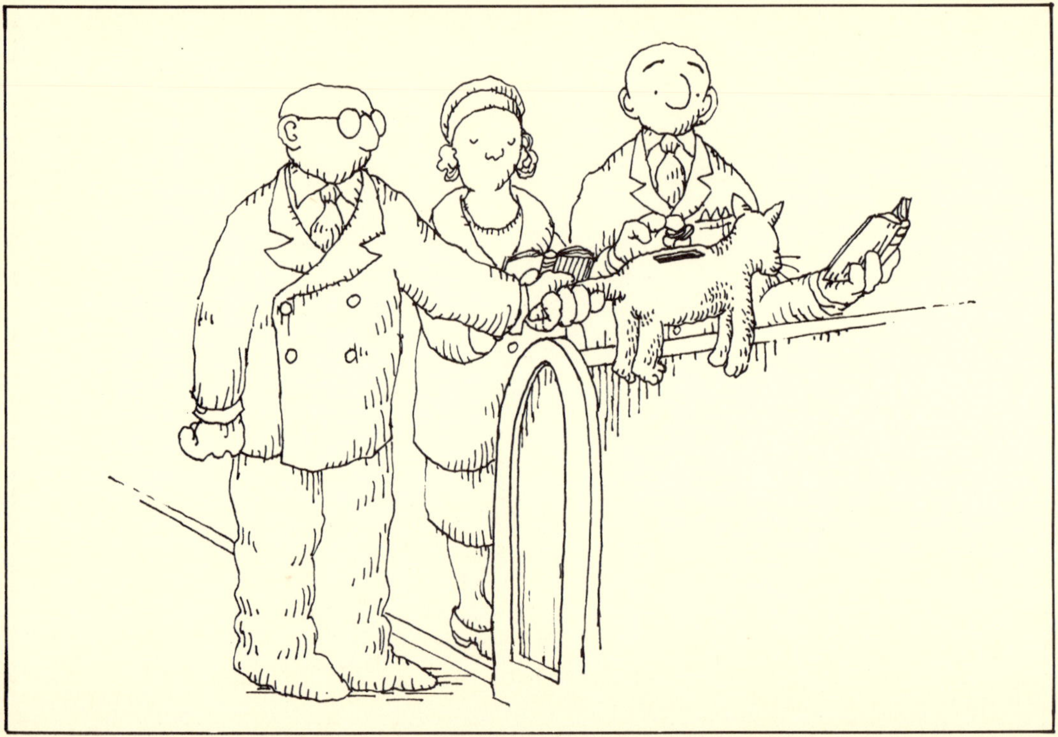

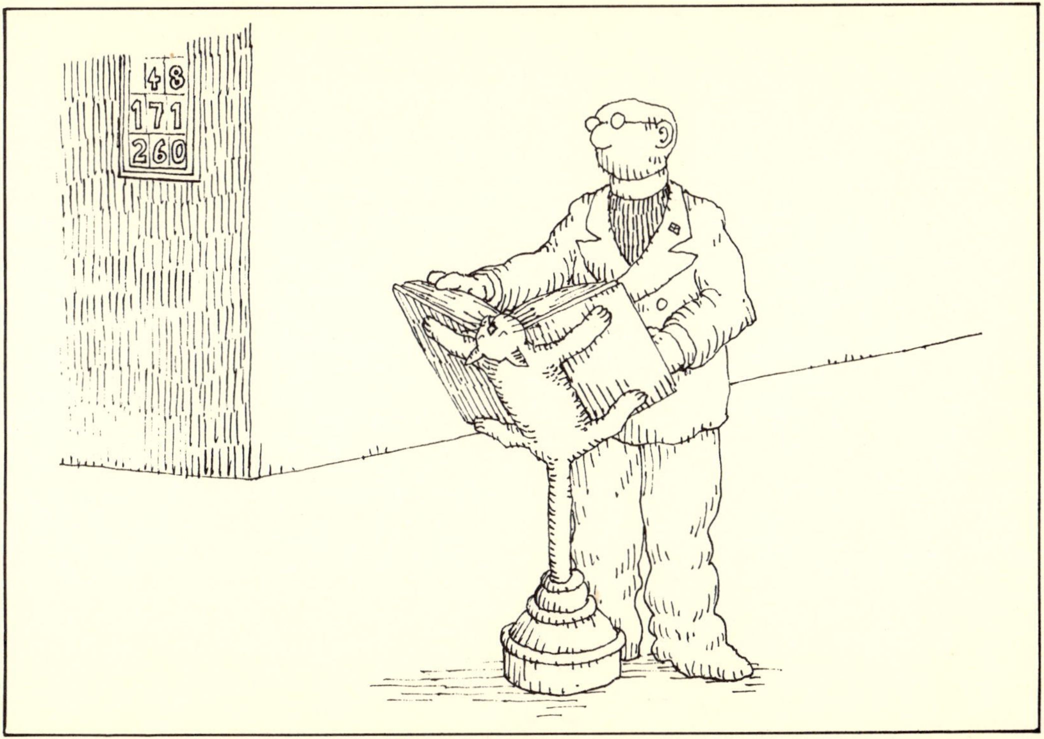
48
171
260

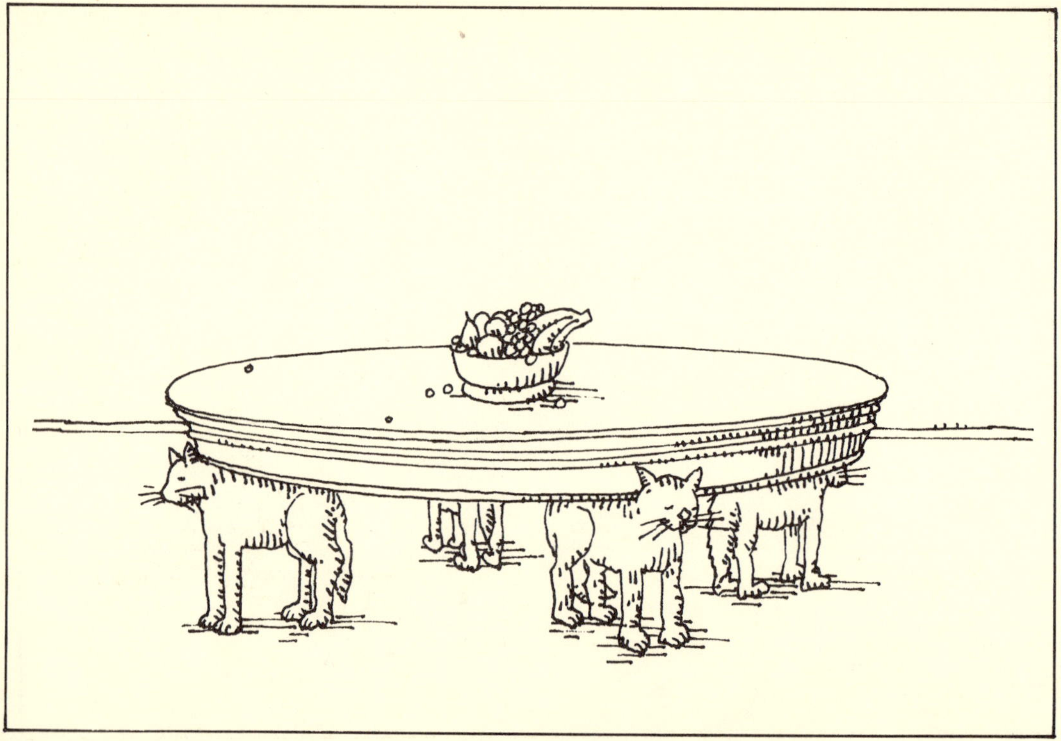

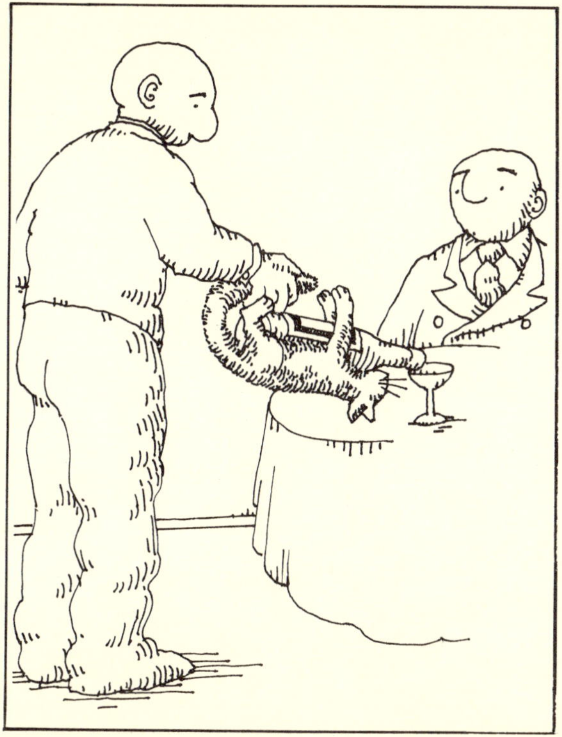

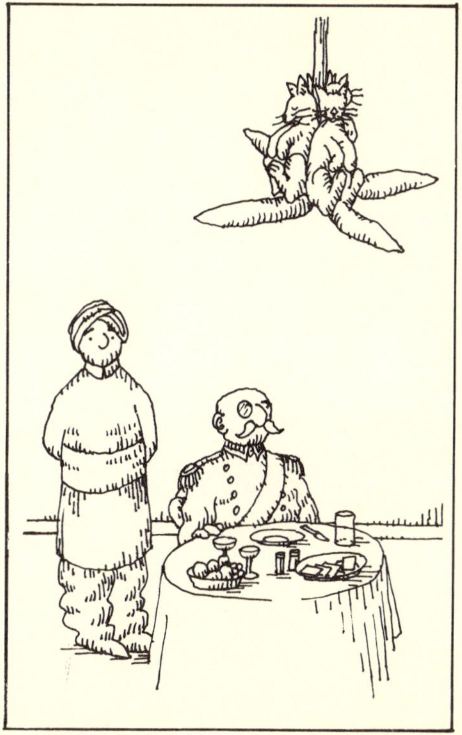

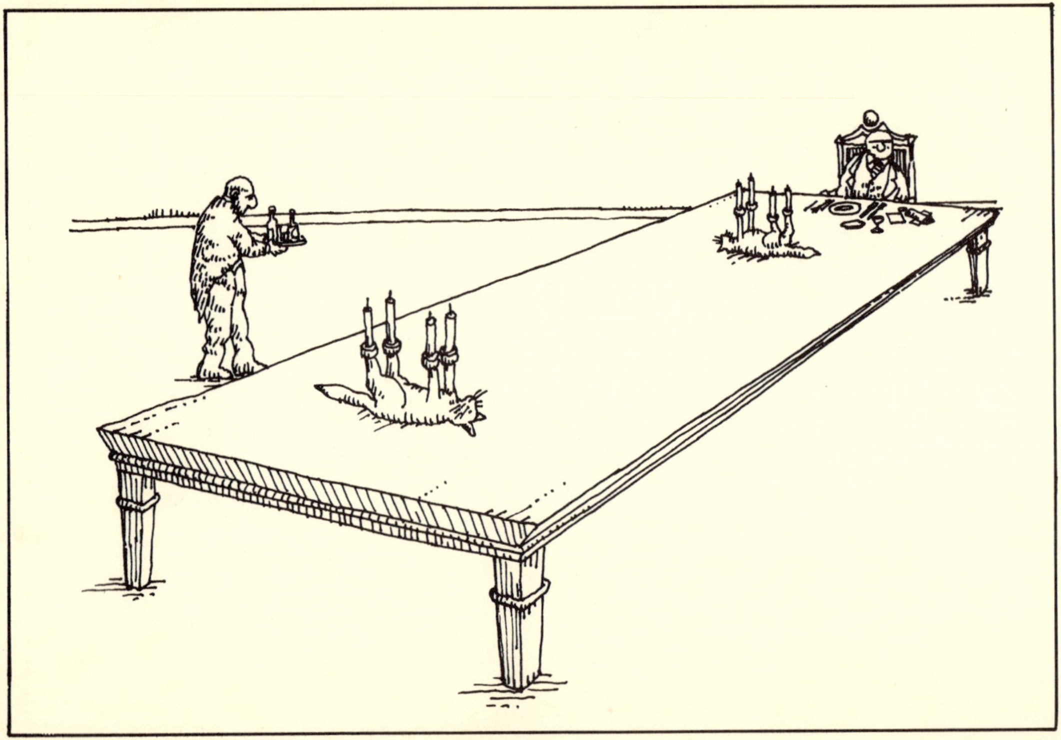

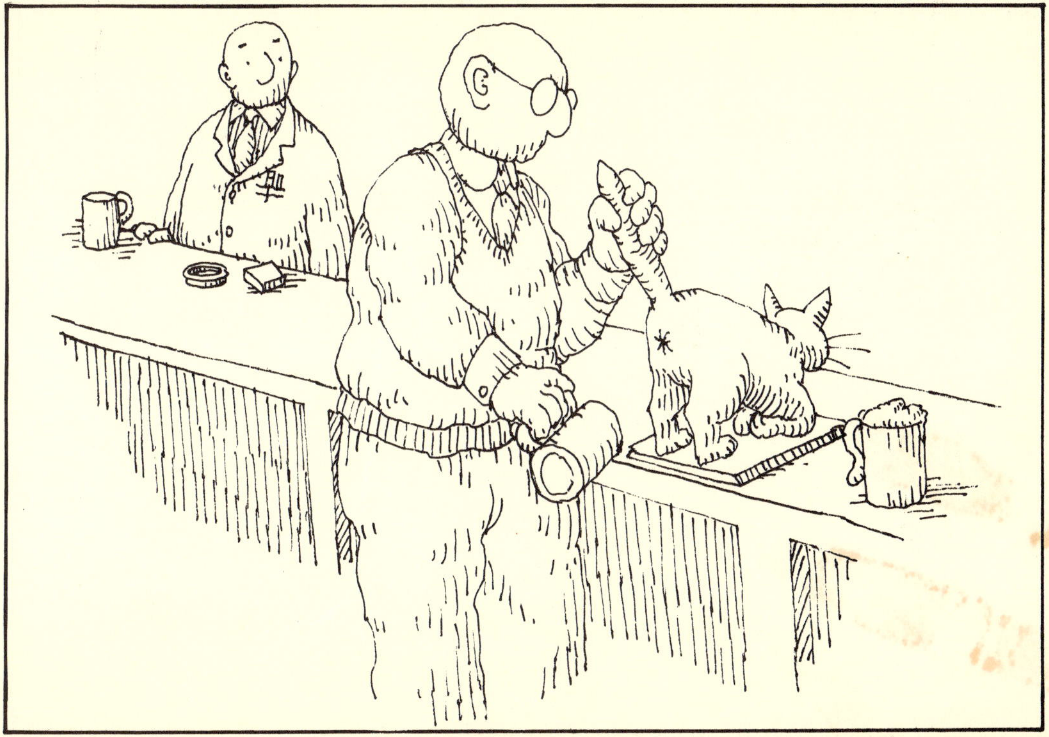

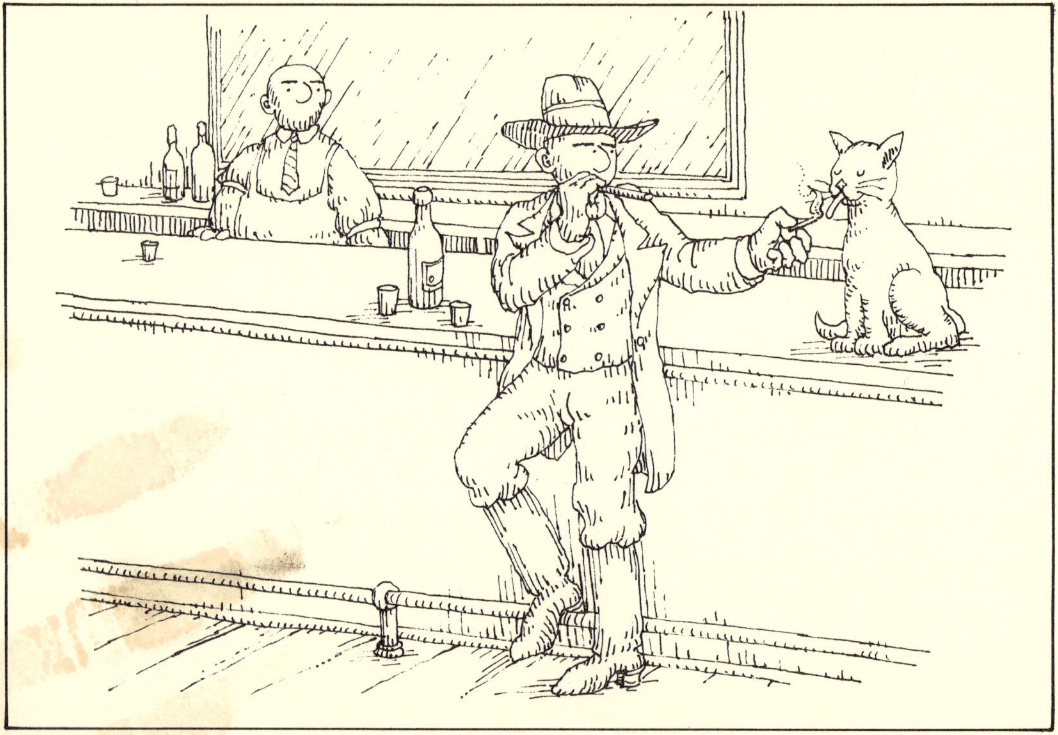

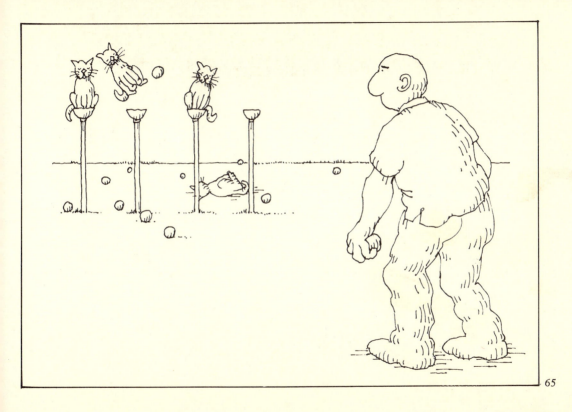

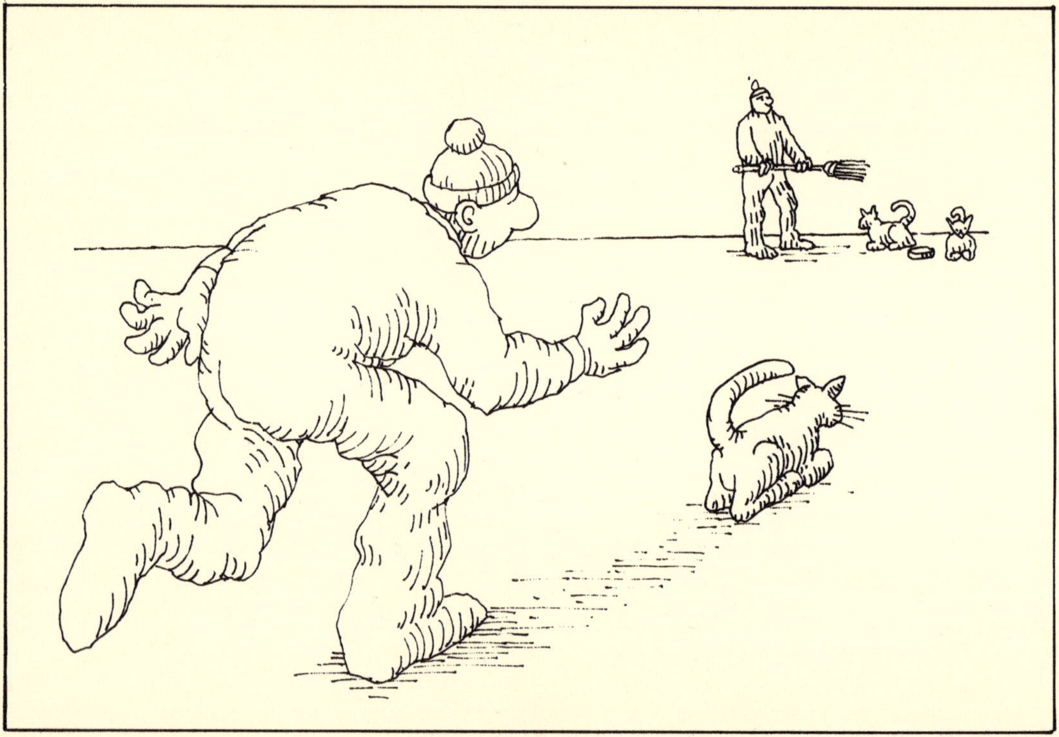

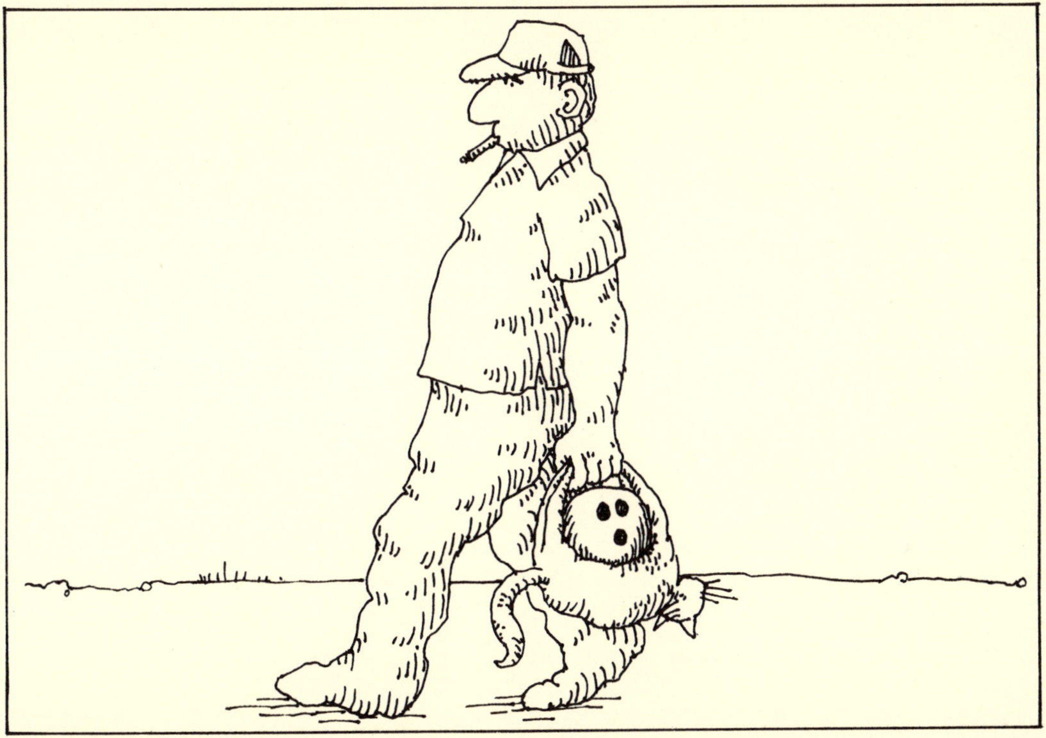

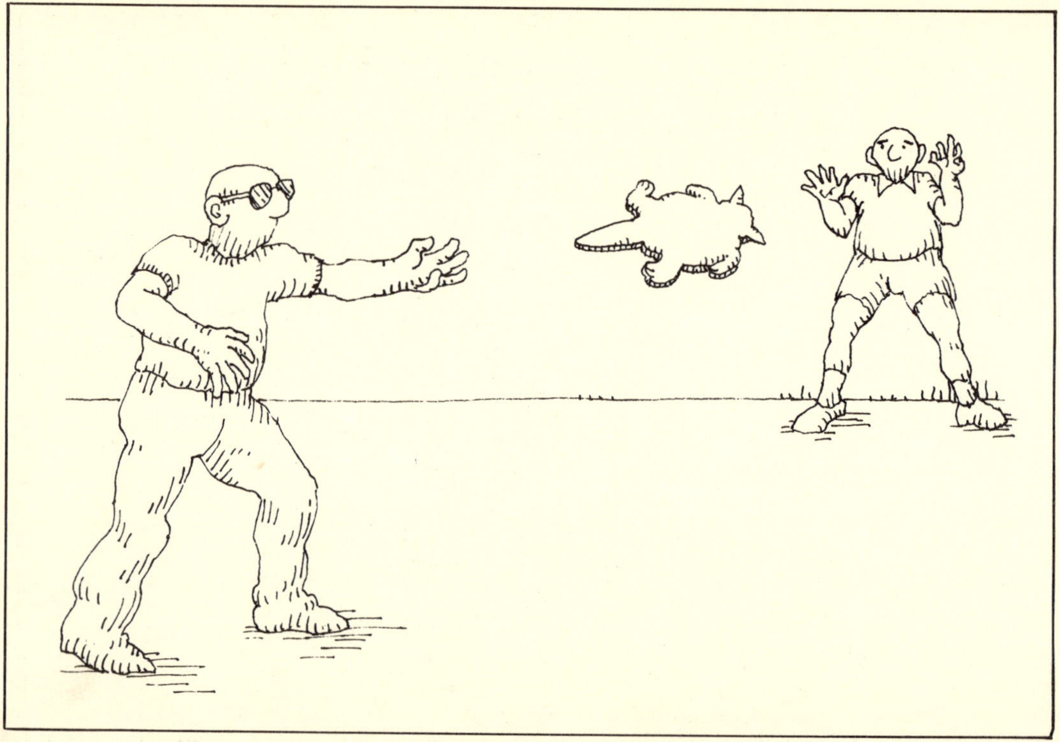

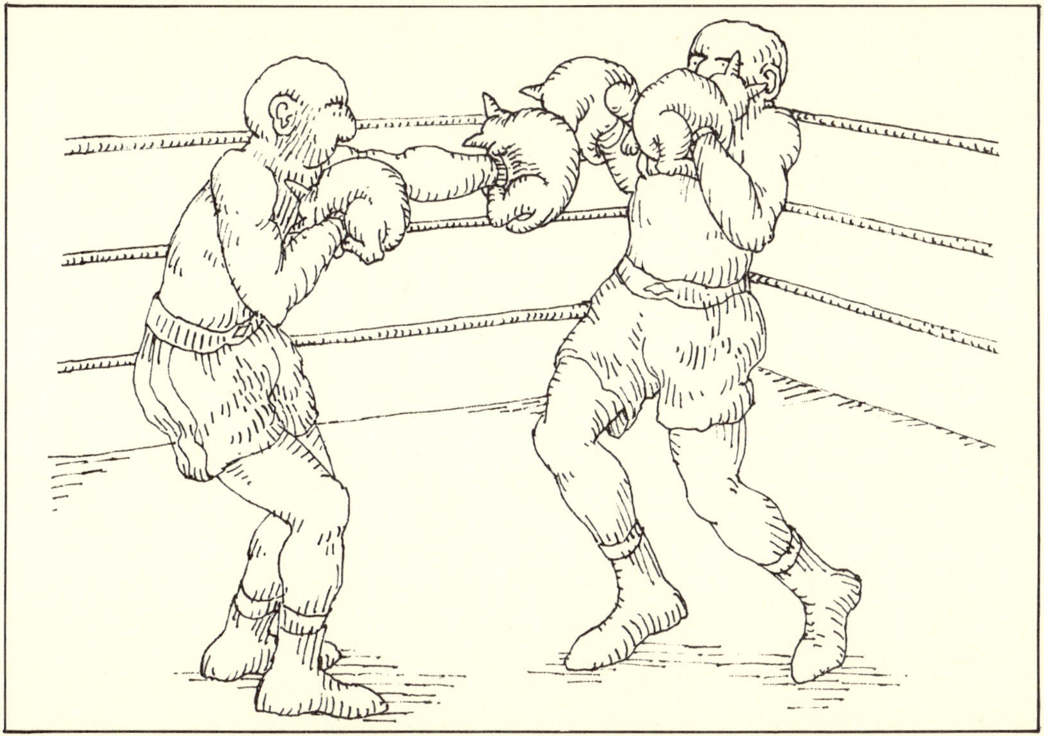

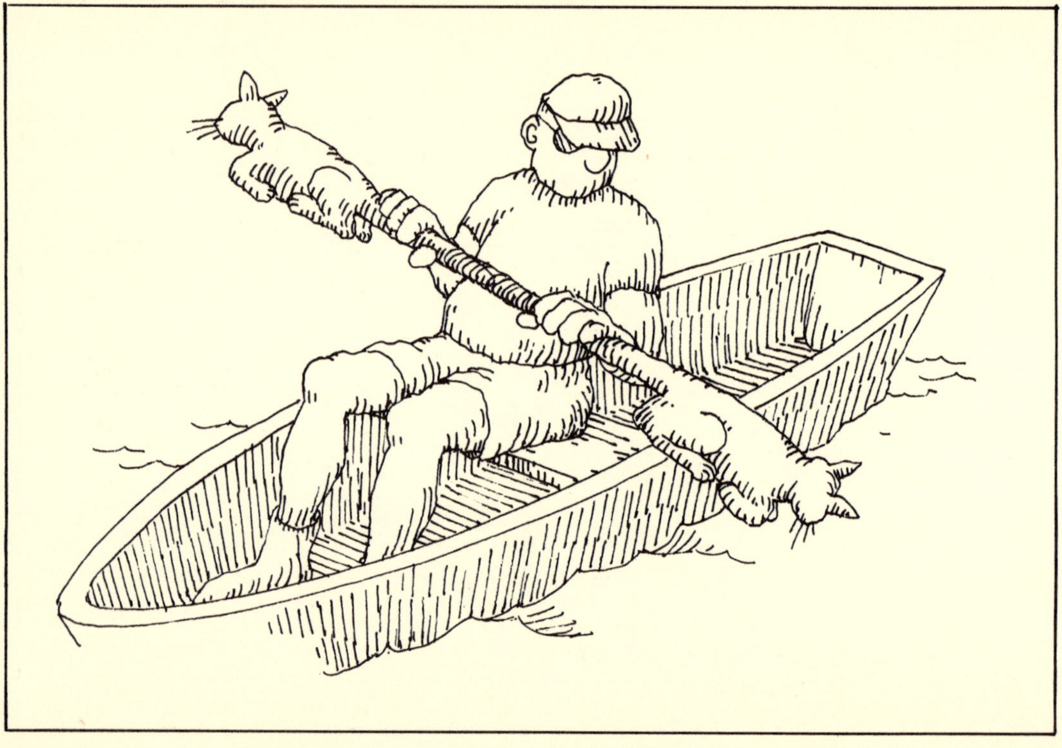

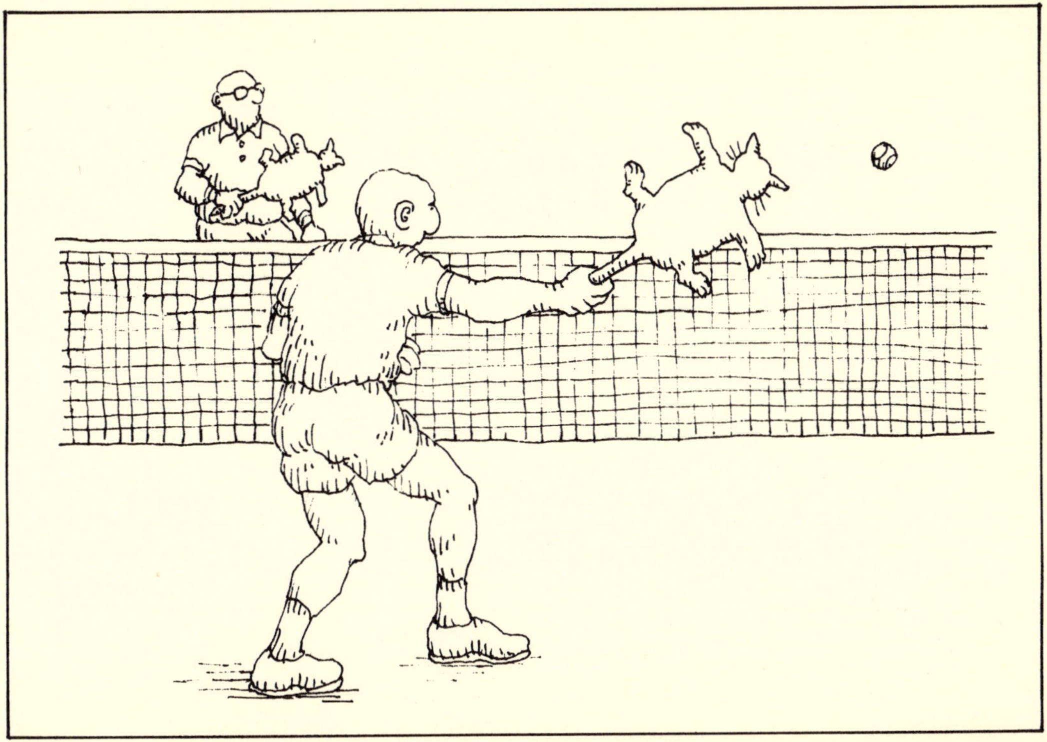

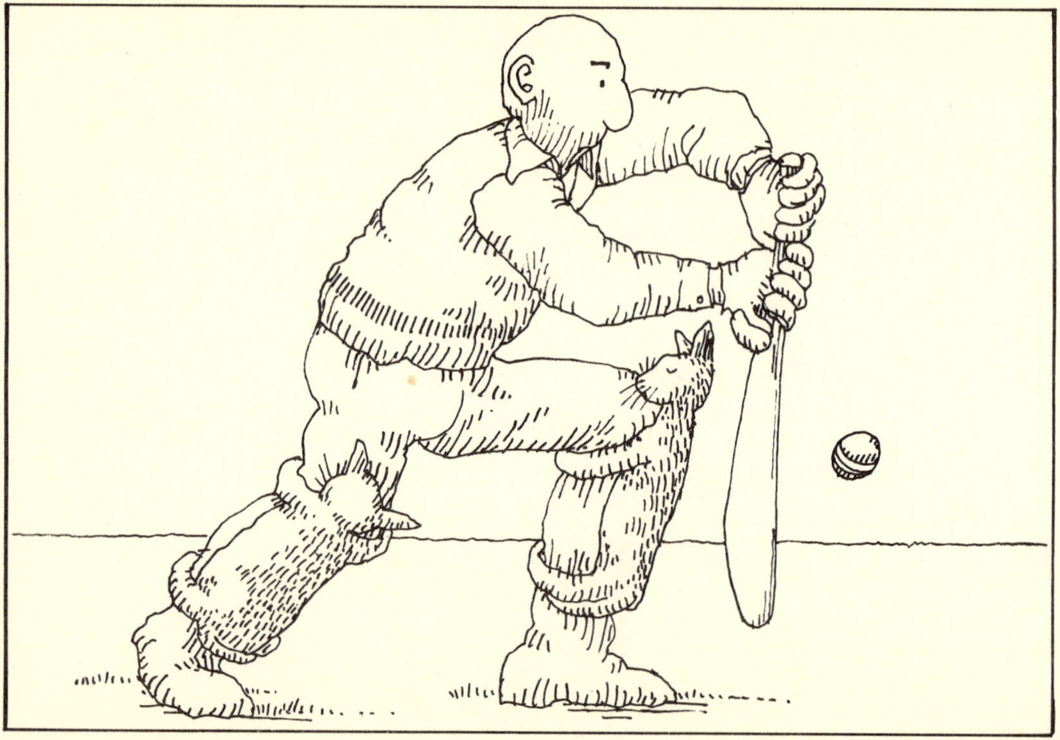

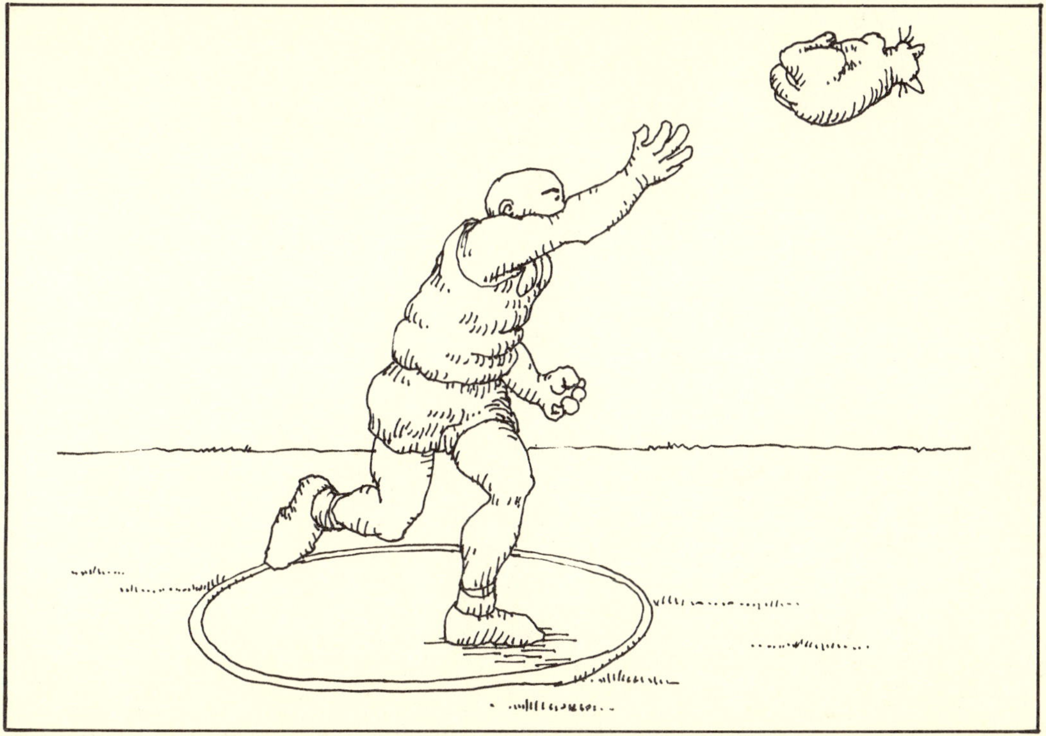

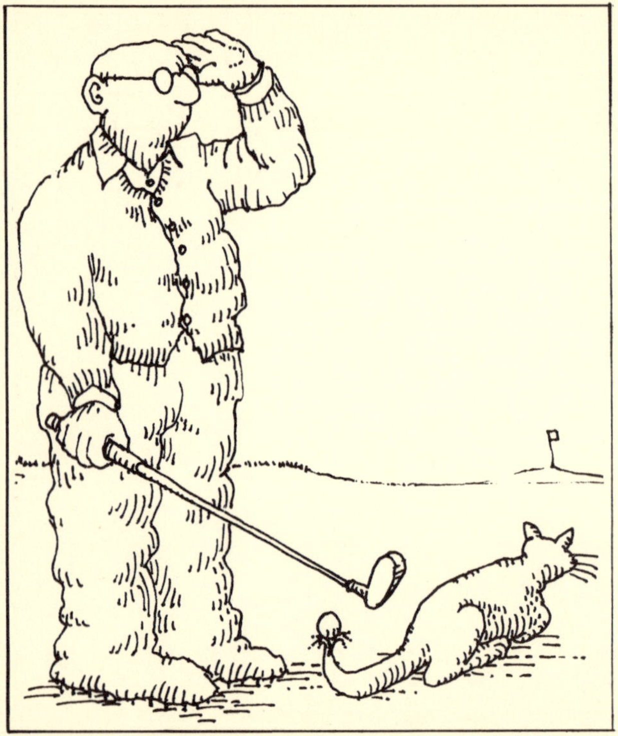

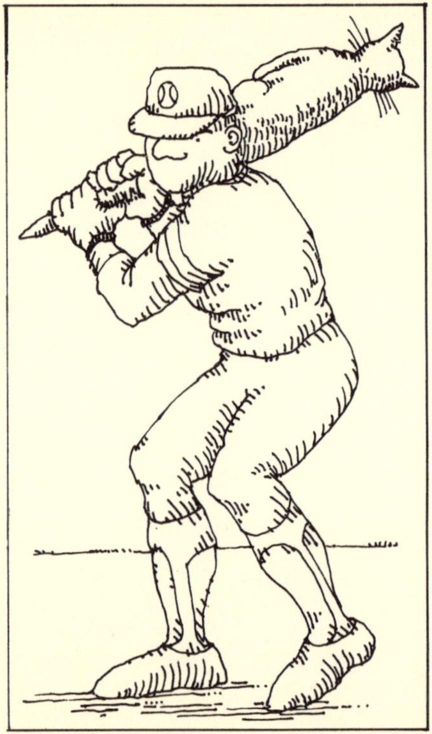

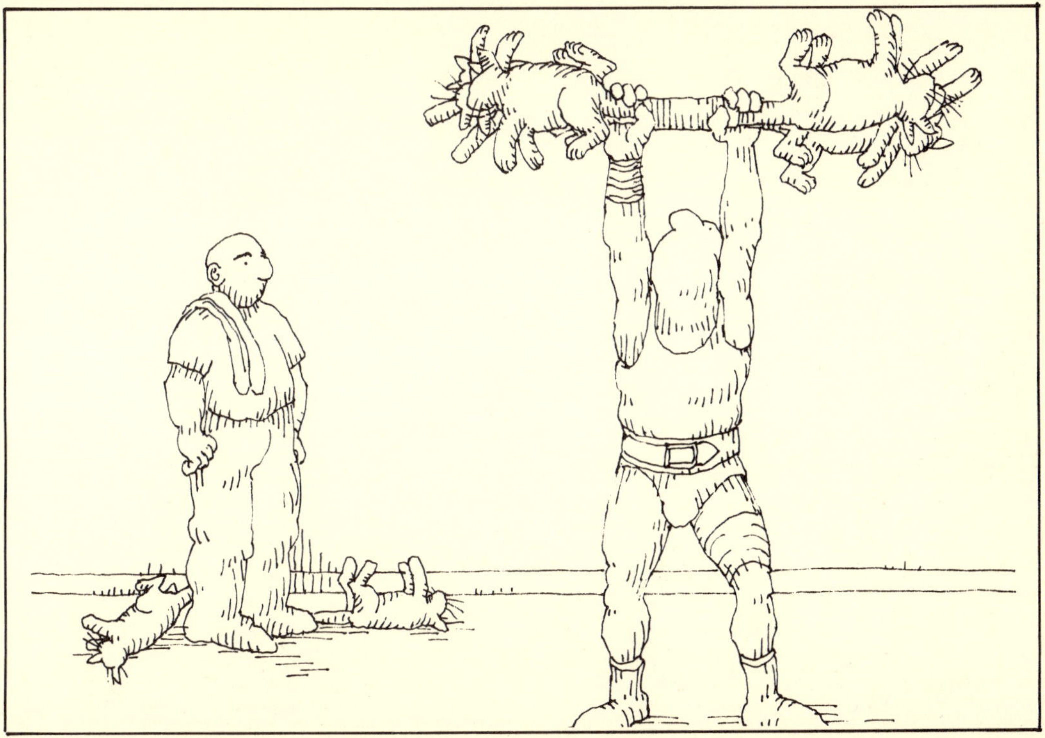

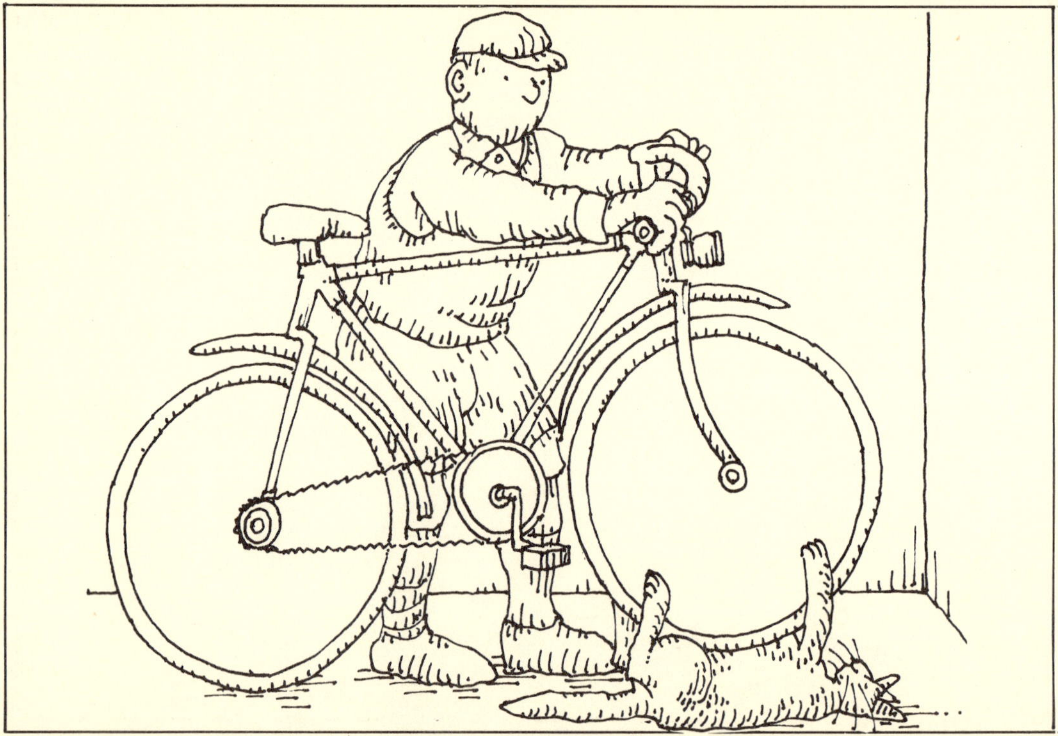

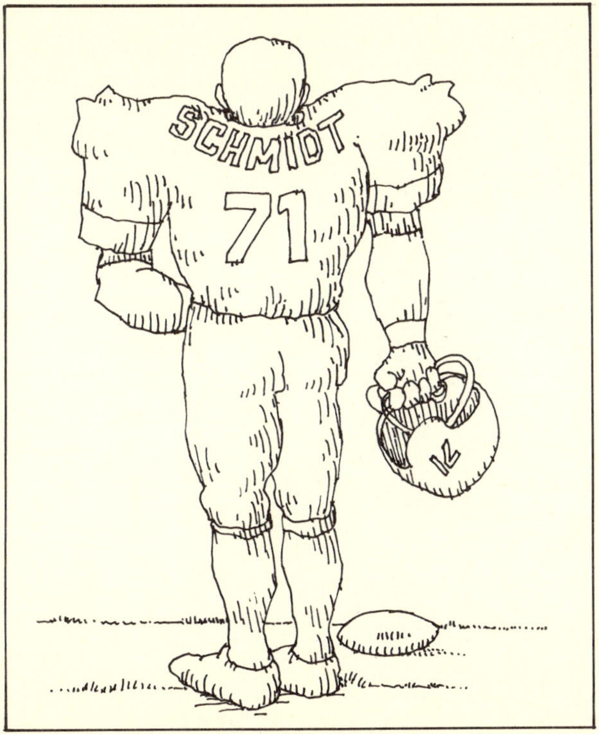
SCHMIDT
71

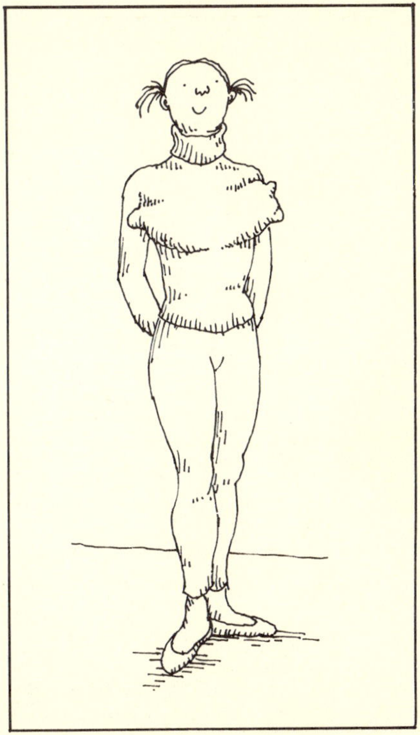

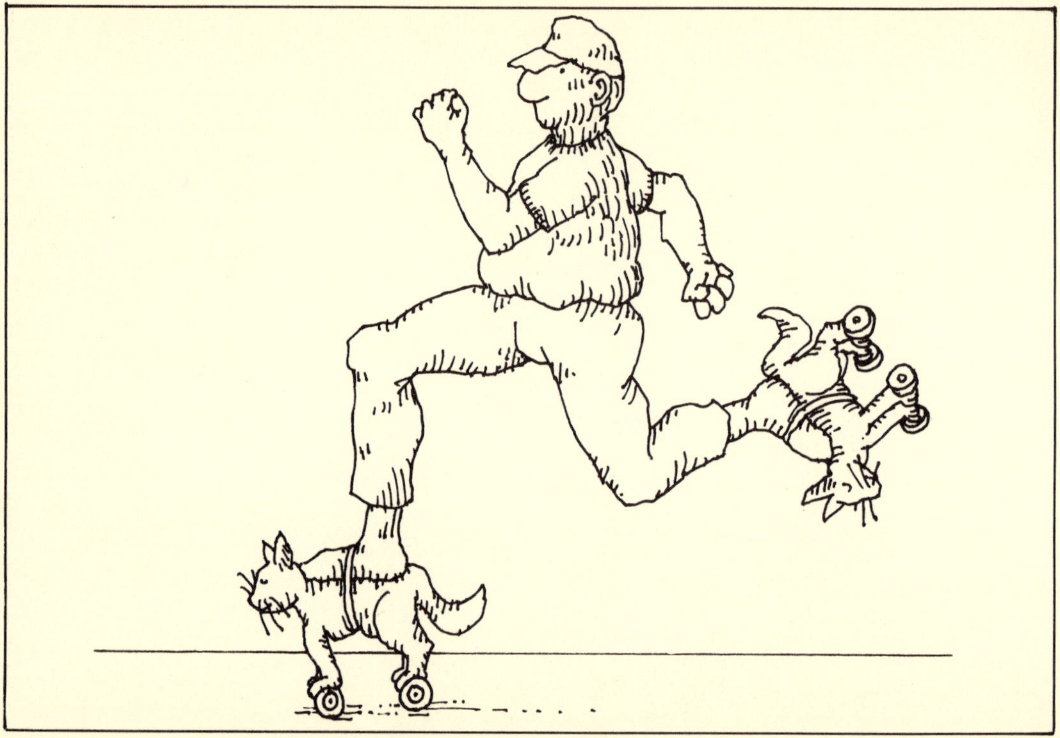

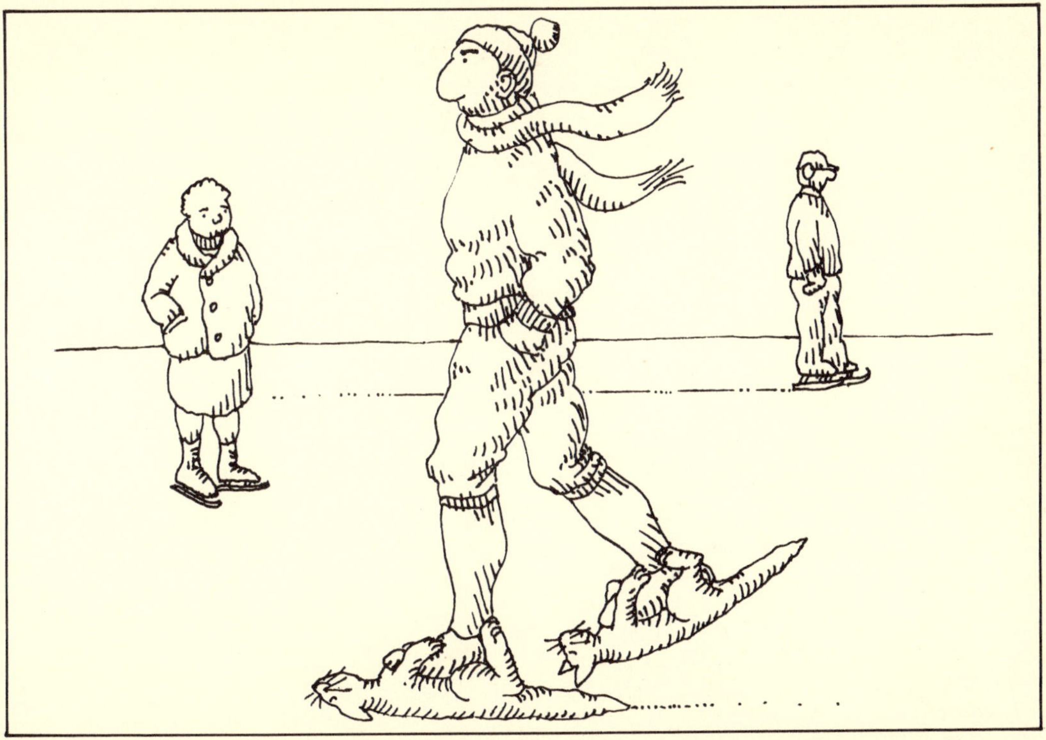

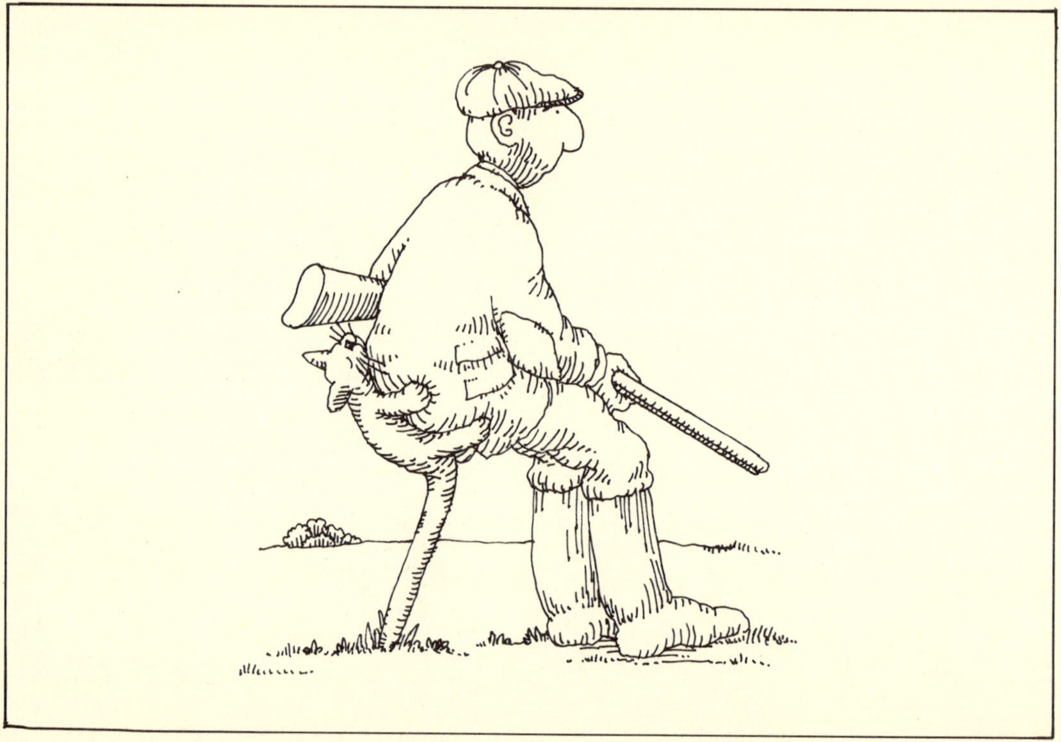

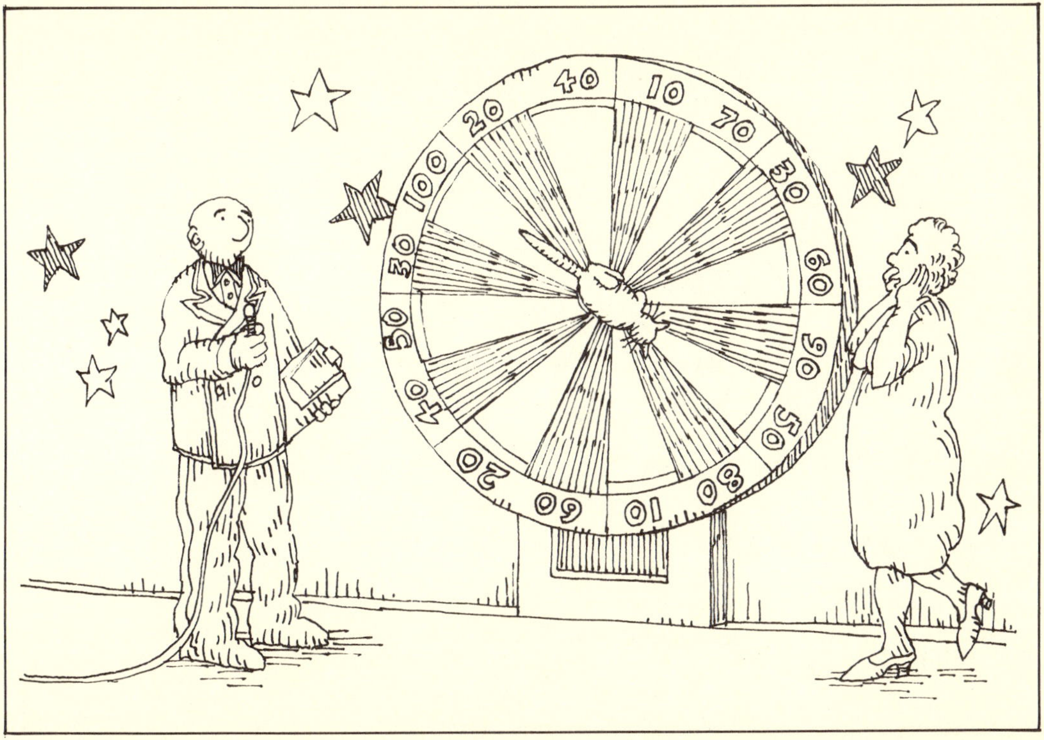
40
10
70
30
60
90
50
80
10
60
20
40
50
30
100
20

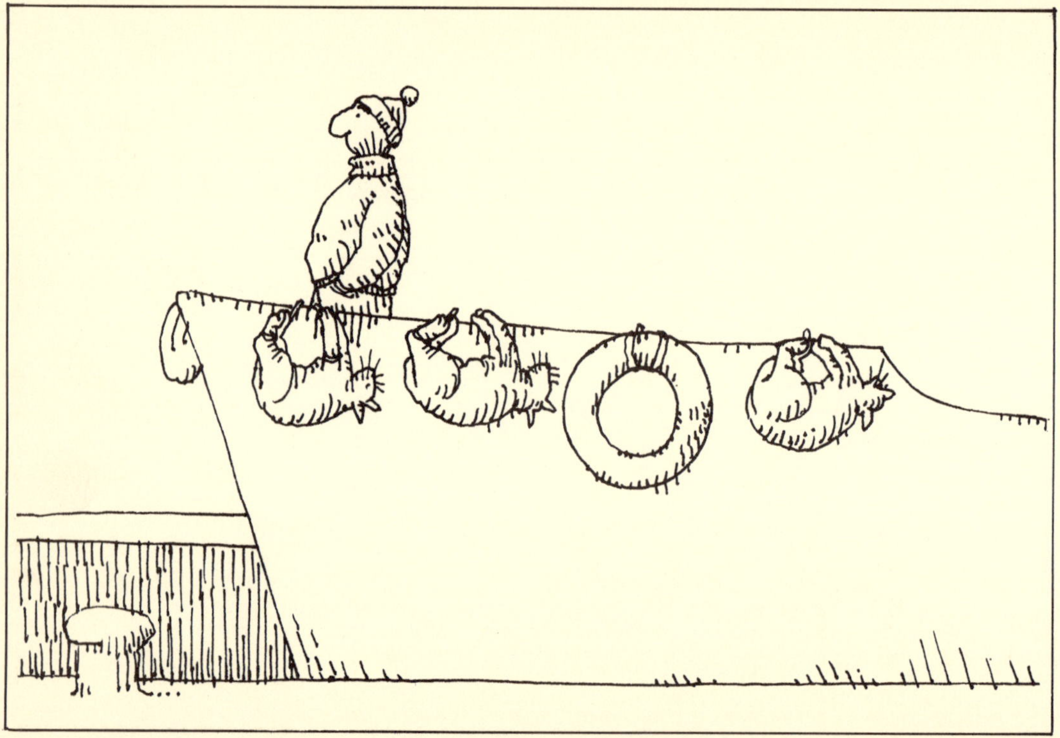

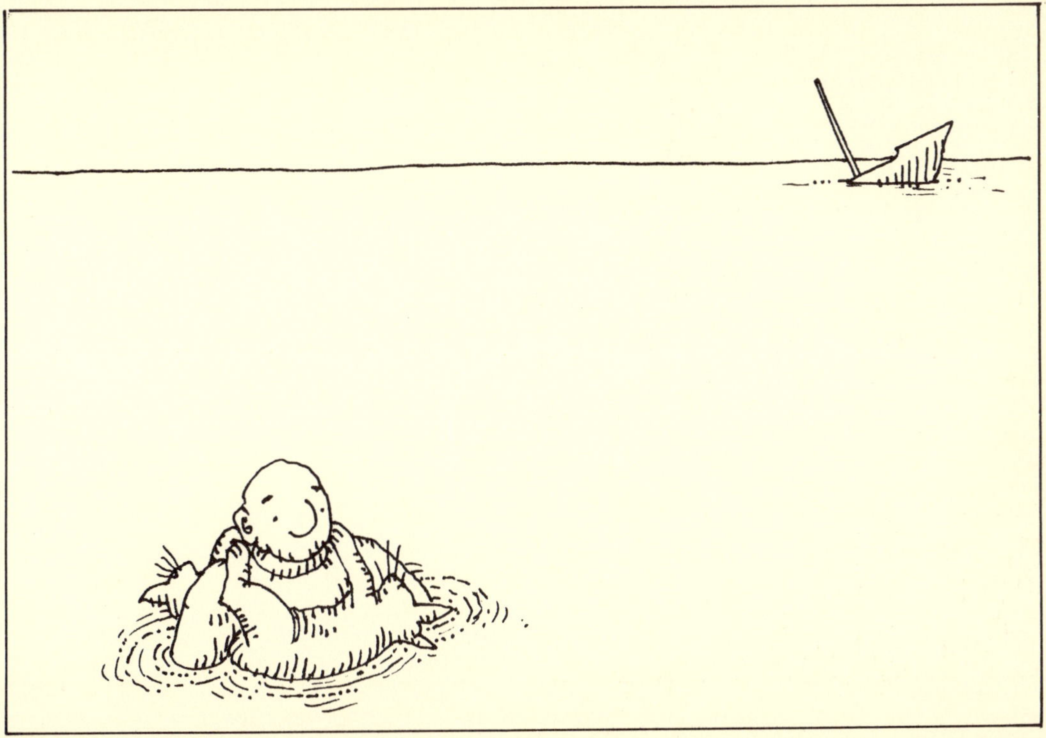

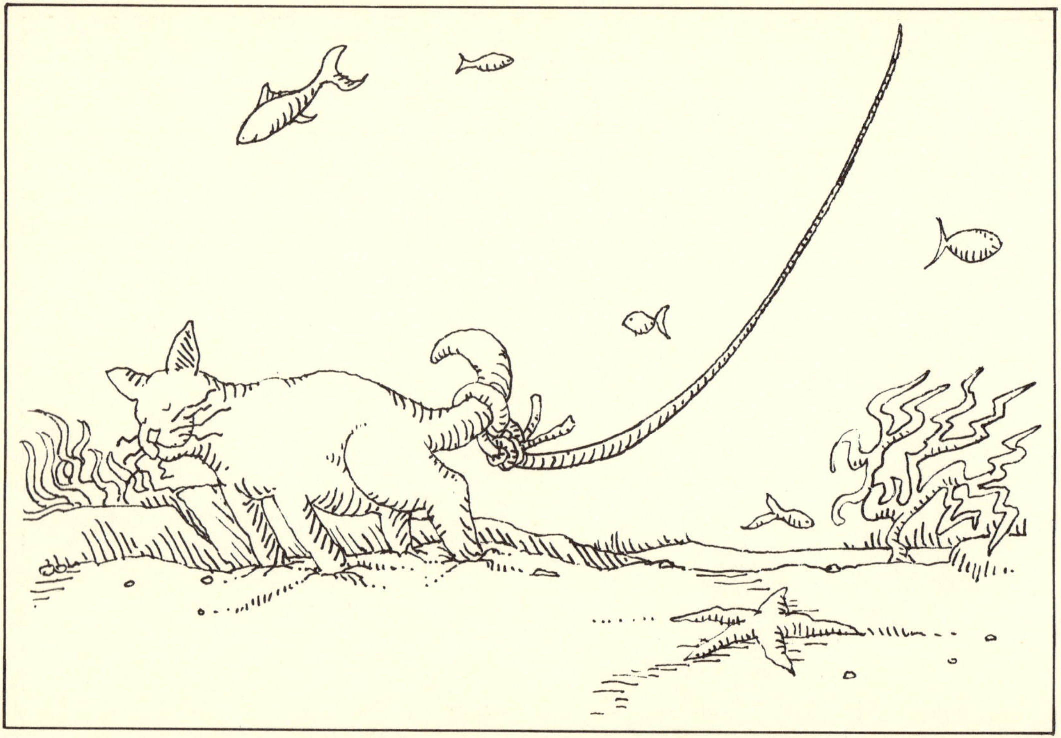

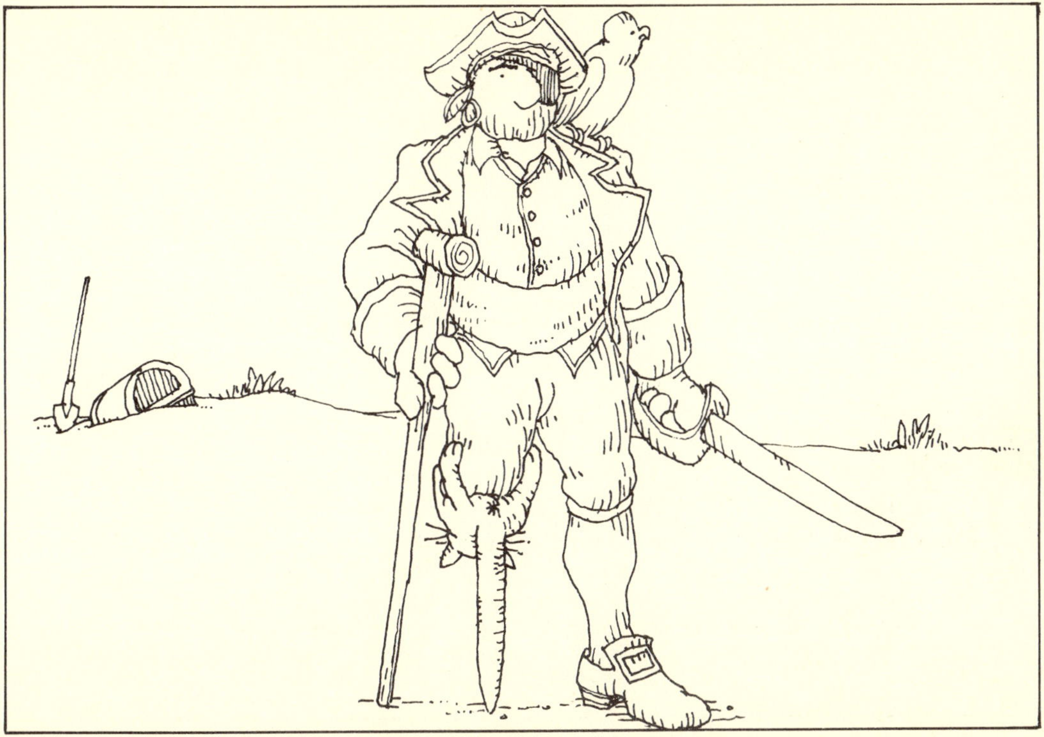

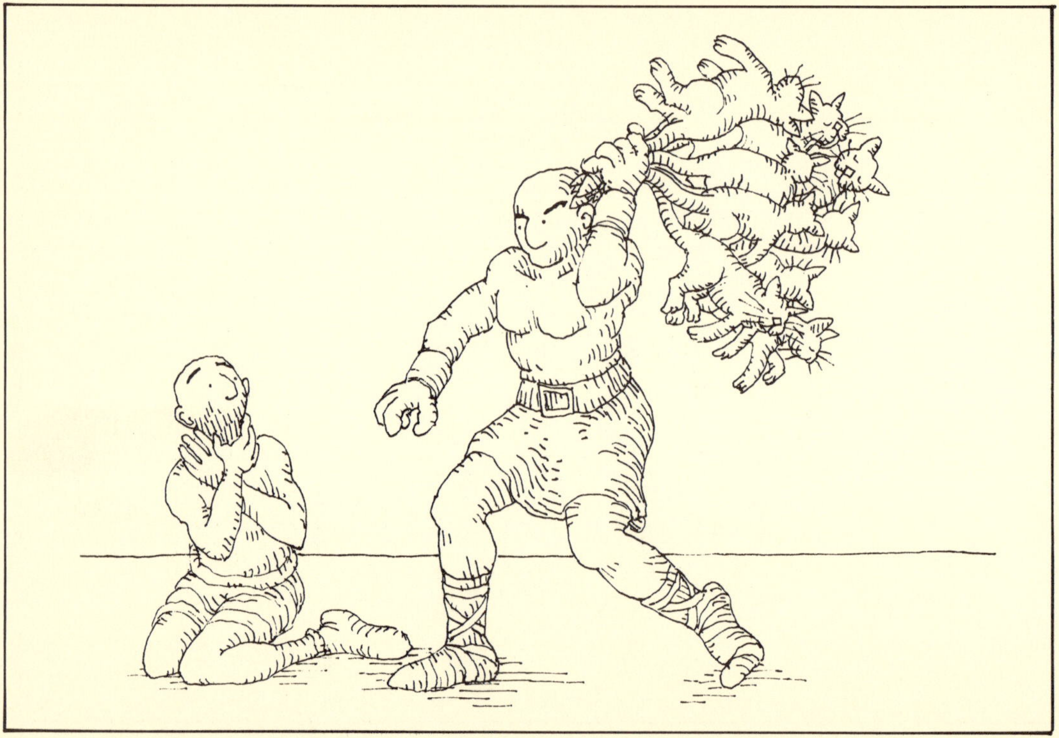

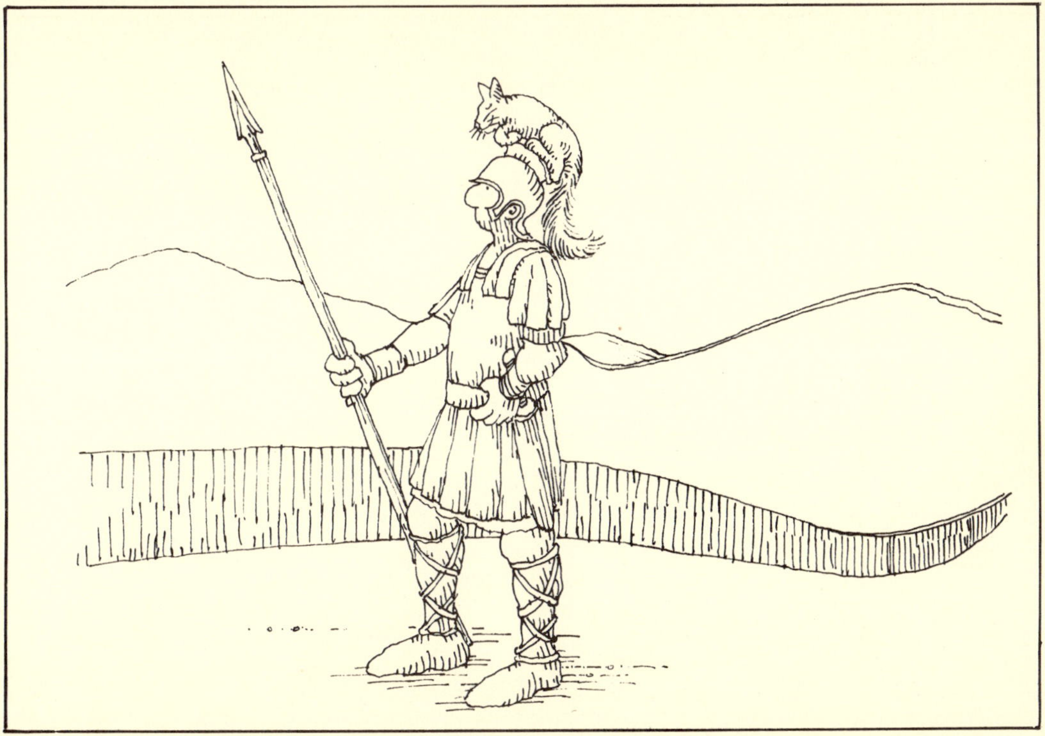

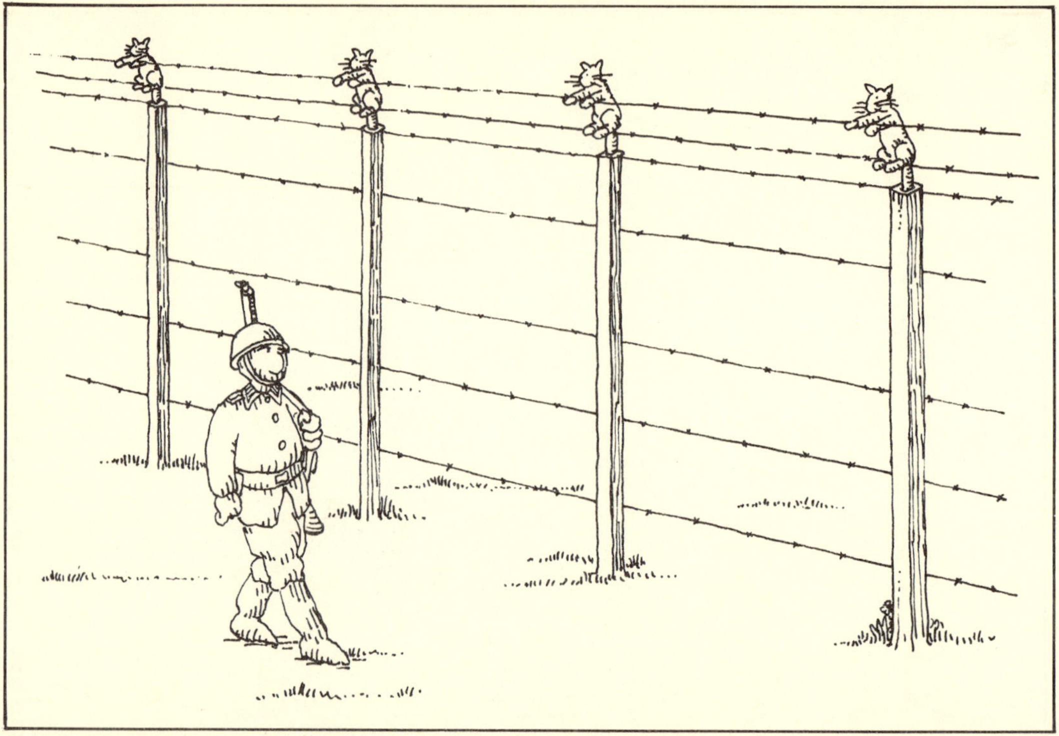

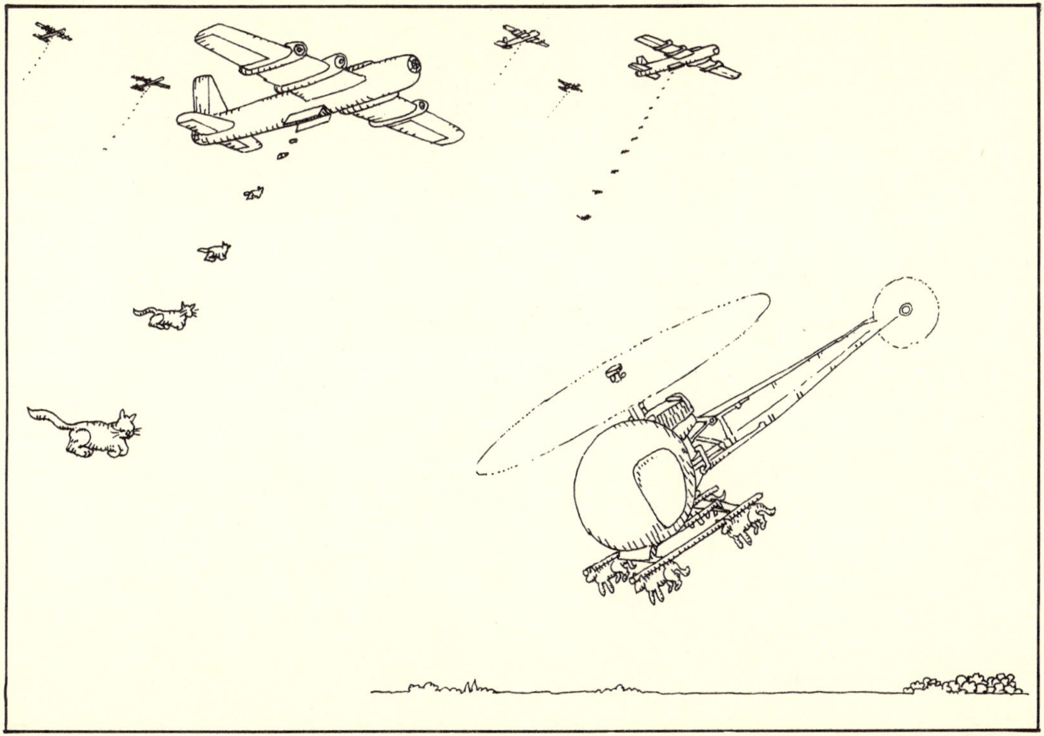

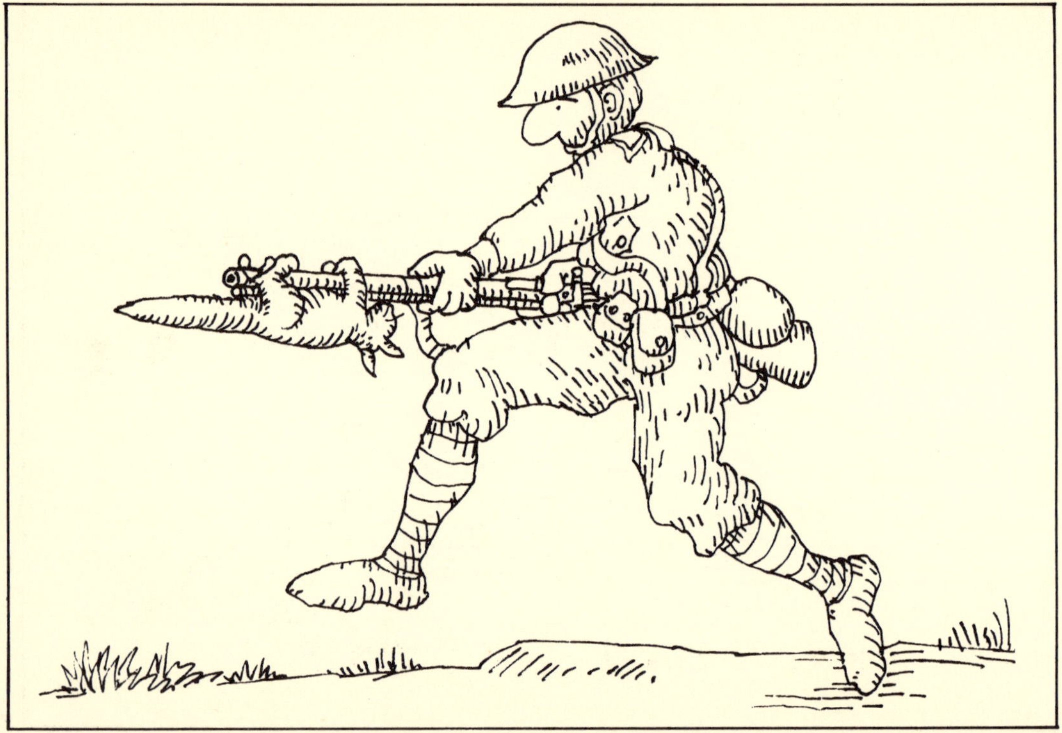

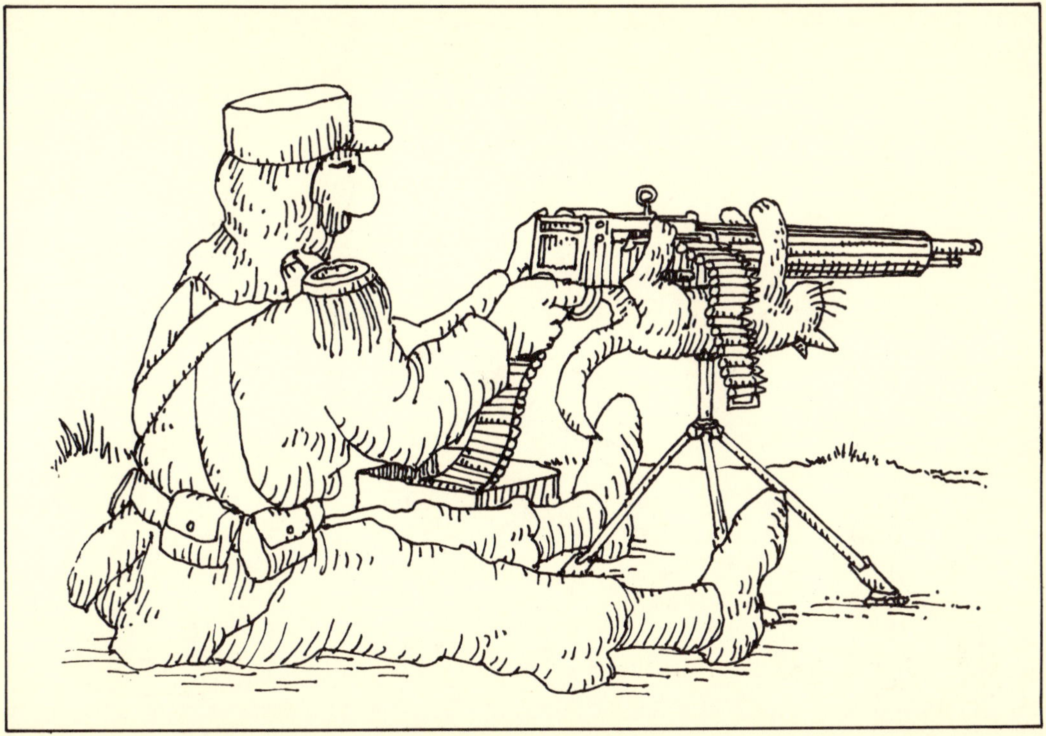

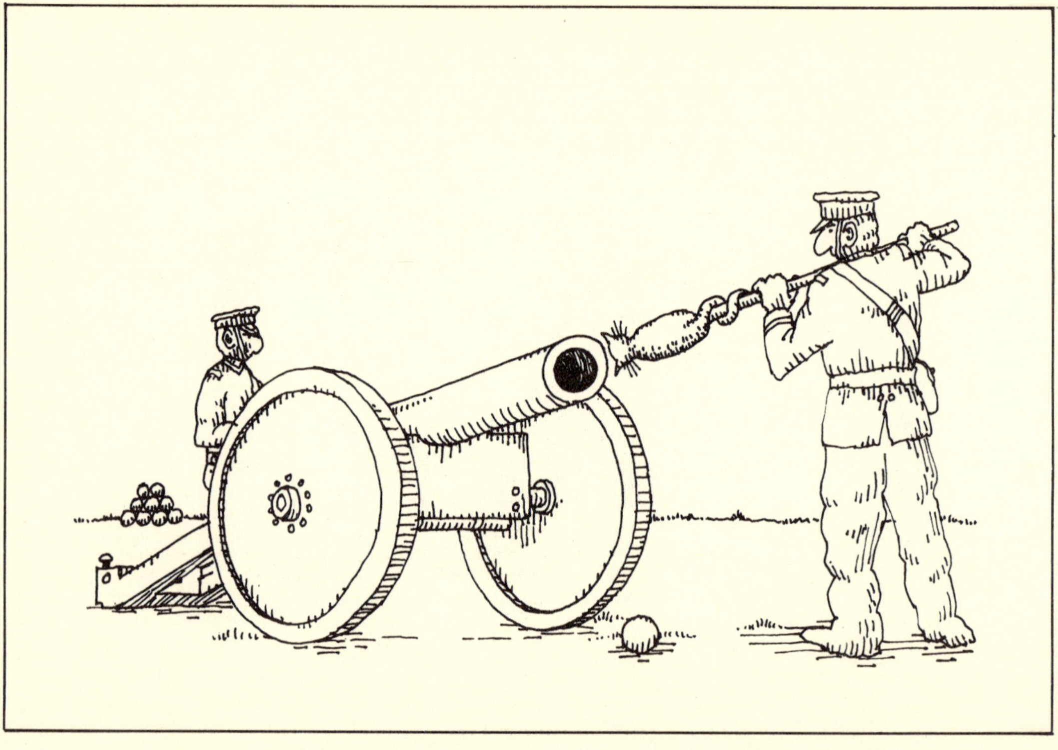

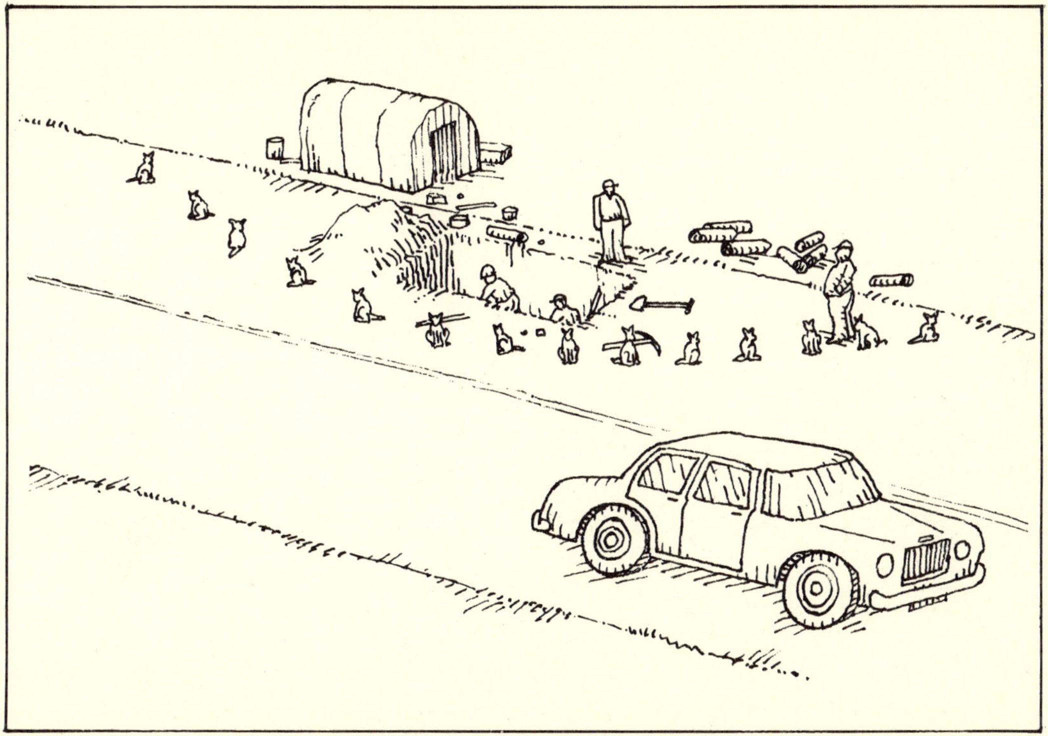

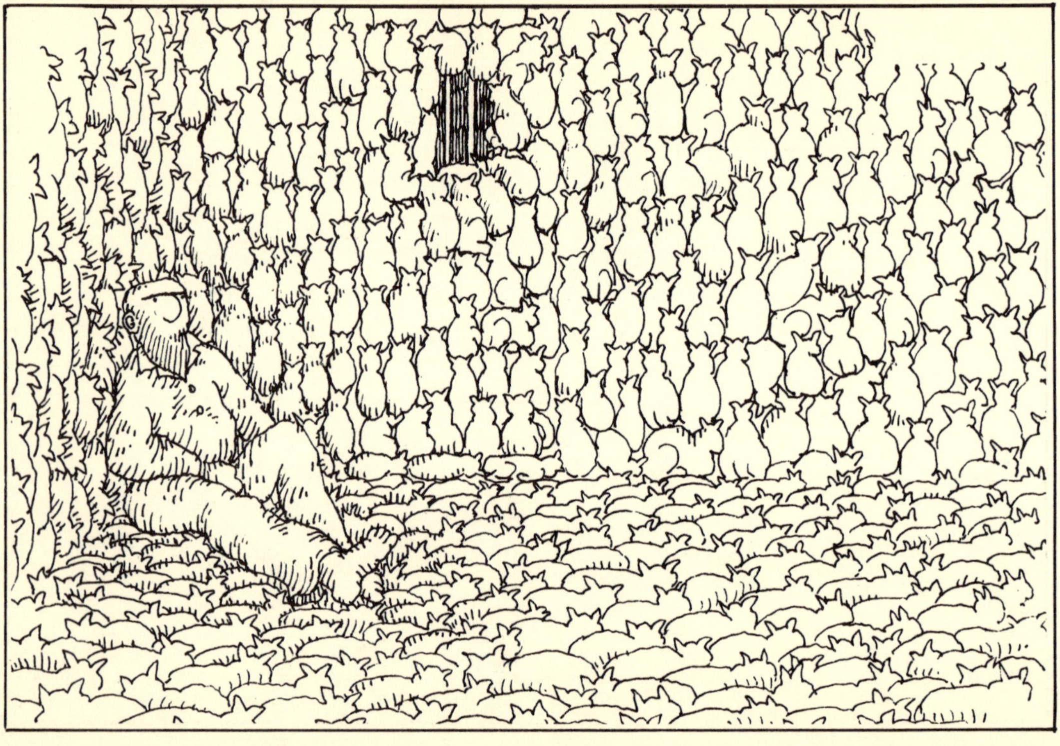

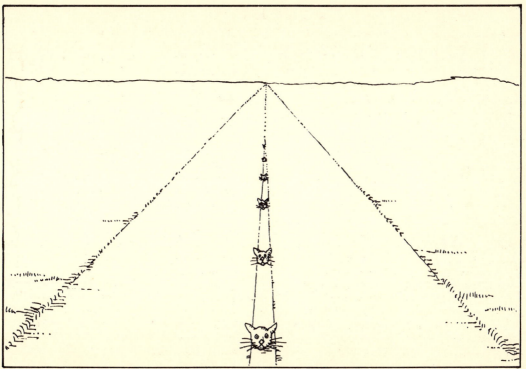

Index of Uses

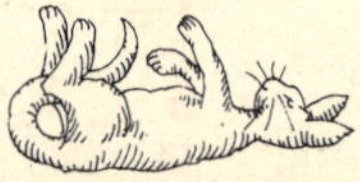